The Meaning of Civilisation

Essays on Culture, Religion and Politics

The Non-Fiction Writing of Naguib Mahfouz Volume II

في ذكرى

مارك لينز

'As a citizen Naguib Mahfouz sees civility and the continuity of a transnational, abiding, Egyptian personality in his work as perhaps surviving the debilitating processes of conflict and historical degeneration which he, more than anyone else I have read, has so powerfully depicted.'

—Edward Said

'One of the greatest creative talents in the realm of the novel in the world.'

—Nadine Gordimer

'He is not only a Hugo and a Dickens, but also a Galsworthy, a Mann, a Zola, and a Jules Romain.'

—*London Review of Books*

'Mahfouz embodied the essence of what makes the bruising, raucous, chaotic human anthill of Cairo possible.'

—*The Economist*

NAGUIB MAHFOUZ

The Meaning of Civilisation

Essays on Culture, Religion and Politics

The Non-Fiction Writing of Naguib Mahfouz Volume II

Introduction by Rasheed El-Enany
Translated by Aran Byrne and Russell Harris

SPEAKING
TIGER

SPEAKING TIGER PUBLISHING PVT. LTD
4381/4 Ansari Road, Daryaganj,
New Delhi–110002, India

Originally published in Arabic by *Dar Al Masriah Al Lubnaniah* 2015

First published in English as *Essays on the Sadat Era (197–1981)*
in the United Kingdom by Gingko Library, 2017
First published in India as *The Meaning of Civilisation:
Essays on Culture, Religion and Politics* by Speaking Tiger, 2017

This edition published in arrangement with
The Gingko Library
70 Cadogan Place, London SW1X 9AH

ISBN: 978-93-86702-23-4
eISBN: 978-93-86702-24-1

10 9 8 7 6 5 4 3 2 1

Printed at Gopsons Papers Ltd

Contents

Introduction

by Rasheed El-Enany

The volume to hand contains the essays of three separate volumes originally published in Arabic, namely *On Culture and Education* (1990); *On Religion and Democracy* (1990); and *On Youth and Freedom* (1990). They represent the first collections of Mahfouz's short current-affairs column in the Egyptian daily, *Al Ahram*, published weekly with the generic title *wijhat nazar* or 'a point of view'. The volume to hand adopts a chronological arrangement of the essays, unlike the Arabic volumes which attempted three loose thematic groupings as suggested by the titles but at the expense of the chronology restored here. Nor does the current volume contain all the essays in the aforementioned three volumes, since it is limited to the Sadat years when Mahfouz started his column in 1974, and stops at the end of 1981, the year Sadat was assassinated. The rest of the essays will appear chronologically in future volumes of this series of Mahfouz's non-fiction writings.

Some of the essays are rather dated and closely related to the affairs current in their day, and particularly in Egypt, such that they would only make sense to a contemporary of the time of their writing, or a specialist steeped in the study of the period. As such, they are a valuable window into the era that produced them and what Mahfouz thought concerning the happenings of the day. Their greatest fascination for a literary scholar like myself is in comparing these stark expressions of Mahfouz's social and political thought with the same, clad in the intricate texture of his fiction. Questions of uniformity and inconsistency are bound to be of interest. The range of topics is immense in both variety and range: political pluralism; religious education; overstaffing in government departments; corruption; film censorship; elections; scientific research; public morality; Egypt's debts; authors' rights and piracy, etc. In what follows, I shall offer some disparate observations that arise from reading this vast number of little essays.

Mahfouz can fall into oversimplification as when in the article 'Religion and School' he reduces the teaching of religion to that of 'good behaviour' with pupils achieving the highest grade in the subject based on their treatment of their classmates and teachers, etc., not to mention his ignoring of the complex issue of how to teach religion to classes of mixed faith, given that Egyptians are made up of Muslims and Christians. He had treated the complexity of this issue beautifully in a short story titled *'Jannat al-Atfal*□ or 'Children's Heaven', from the collection *Khammarat al-Qitt al-Aswad* or 'Black Cat Tavern' (1969) where a hapless father reels under the innocent but ruthless investigation by his little girl on why she and her Christian best friend have to be separated during religion classes at school. The sensitivity shown in the fictional treatment is lost in the article without trace.

Worse still is when Mahfouz falls into self-contradiction. In an article titled 'Islam and the Battle of Ideologies', he puts Islam on a par with 'Western democracy' on the one hand, and 'communism' on the other, and goes on to make comparisons between the three ideologies. He even talks of the 'economic model' of Islam and how it differs from 'capitalism', and falls into the naïve identification of the concept of *shura* or 'consultation [in affairs of government]' in Islam with Western democracy. In doing this he falls unwittingly into the trap of accepting that Islam is not just a religion but a complete socio-political system, something that goes against the grain of his vast novelistic representations to the contrary, not least in his magnum opus, *The Cairo Trilogy,* where the Muslim Brotherhood, the rising political force of the 1930s and 1940s is ridiculed as an irrelevancy in modern times. Only two weeks later, apparently in response to some readers' letters, we find him backtracking in an article titled 'O God!', arguing that modern man should expect no new revelation from heaven but must make rationality alone the true human means to knowledge. This is more like the Mahfouz we know from his fiction than in the above essay.

Some turns of phrase in these short essays can display a harshness and a cynicism totally uncharacteristic of Mahfouz both as person and as writer, as when he closes an essay on corruption, 'Millions and Pennies', written at the time of Sadat's early attempts at political liberalization, by wondering whether the nation at that moment of its life and in the face or rampant corruption was more in need of policemen, informers, prisons and gallows than of political platforms or parties.

Conversely, his essays can also reflect more blatantly his originality of thought, experimental spirit, and readiness to question received opinion that we have witnessed in his fiction time and again, if often behind a symbolic structure or a metaphorical narrative. In an essay titled 'Killing your Brother whether He is a Criminal or a Victim', written in June 1976 in the nascent years of the Lebanese Civil War (1975–90), we hear Mahfouz admonishing the Palestinians, albeit respectfully, regarding their role in the war, blaming them for having become a state within a state, and reminding them of what he sees as the same role they had previously played in Jordan, which led to the infamous war between them and the Jordanian state in 1970, often referred to as the Black September. Such a stance was not an easy one to take at the time. Progressive writers were supposed to support the Palestinians regardless and to denounce the Lebanese Maronites as a force of reaction. It must have taken courage for Mahfouz to adopt such a position. This can be seen as an indicator of a much more controversial stance that Mahfouz was to take later in support of Sadat's peace initiative with Israel in 1977 and the following years against the almost unanimous outcry of the intellectual class in Egypt at the time, not to mention the Arab regimes that sought to ostracise Egypt with the removal of the Arab League headquarters from Cairo to Tunis. In this regard we see him in an essay titled 'Diagnosing Calamity' (1/2/1981) railing at those who ignore that conflicts between nations can be solved either by war or negotiation, but not by a state of 'no war, no peace', which seemed to be the favourite 'solution' of those who opposed Egypt's peace accords with Israel.

Similarly, on 20 December 1976, he calls unabashedly on oil-rich Arab countries to pay back Egypt's international debts and to invest their wealth in Egypt instead of the West, reminding them of Egypt's wars on behalf of itself and them. It is interesting to note with the benefit of hindsight that that essay, 'The Philosophy of the State Radio and Television', was written only weeks before the famous bread riots that shook Egypt and Sadat's regime in January 1977, and which erupted when state subsidy was lifted from a variety of essential goods in order to satisfy international monetary conditions for more loans. Later that year Sadat was to visit Israel and address the Knesset in a move that took the world by surprise and alienated Arabs, but which was largely attributed to Egypt's dire economic situation. As already mentioned, Mahfouz was to support the eventual peace accords with Israel of 1979. But ironically, Mahfouz fell silent over the bread riots, an event that shook the nation and nearly toppled the regime. After regaining control, Sadat ridiculed the popular uprising and labelled it 'the thieves' uprising' in a reference to the plundering of posh shops and clubs by the mob that accompanied some of its events. As the contents of this volume show, on this Mahfouz preferred to maintain judicious silence.

Some of Mahfouz's views are hard to accept as genuine, such as what appears to be his taking seriously Sadat's decorative political reforms and the reintroduction of political parties, banned under Nasser, and freedom of the press, also censored under Nasser. He even has praise for the National Party (see his essay 'A Decision of the Majority Party'), which was founded by Sadat and monopolized power through systematic election rigs until discredited and banned more than thirty years later after the ouster of President Mubarak in 2011. What Mahfouz really thought of the Sadat era is not to be found in his weekly column in *Al Ahram*, but in his post-Sadat novel, *The Day the Leader was Killed* (1985), just as we can find what he thought of the Nasser era thinly disguised in the novels of the 1960s during Nasser's heyday, and more explicitly in novels like, *Karnak Café* (1974) and *Before the Throne* (1983), after his death.

Mahfouz's first essay after the assassination of Sadat appeared on its normal date on 12 October 1981, only six days after the murder of the president. Titled 'Eras and Leaders', it is a cold and collected statement of indifference. He offers a sweeping survey of Egypt's leaders since 1952, i.e., Nasser and Sadat, each treated in a short paragraph, writing about the leader murdered six days earlier with the same detachment as about the one who died eleven years before, but most importantly looking forward to the era of the new president, Hosni Mubarak, who had been in power no more than six days, but was already being heralded by Mahfouz as the leader of 'a moral revolution' to put right the rife corruption left behind by Sadat. Little did he know! Nor did he live to see the toppling of Mubarak by a popular revolution that denounced him as a corrupt autocrat.

At a time when Sadat, in his last year in power before his assassination on 6 October 1981, was becoming increasingly and wantonly dictatorial, it is perhaps no wonder that we come across an essay by Mahfouz, titled 'Freedom of Thought' (26/3/1981) where he argues that freedom of thought should be absolute, unfettered by any restraints, and asserts that while free thinking may err, its error can only be rectified by more thought, rather than any external restriction.

But amid the banalities of current affairs and the guarded treading of paths amidst the pages of a state-owned newspaper and the generally straight-jacketed press, one falls occasionally upon a heartfelt piece of writing where the innovative, swimmer-against-the-current Mahfouz is encountered, as in 'Imported Ideas' (10/5/1976). Here he rails against cultural protectionism and illustrates sweepingly from history how, down the ages, cultures were all the time importing and exporting ideas, a process which created progress and civilisation. He goes on to point out the error of imagining that originality or *asala* consisted in loyalty to the legacy of the past and rejection of the foreign, but rather it consisted in 'intellectual independence' from both the traditional and the imported, opting equally for what suited either. In arguing this he was continuing to carry the banner of the conflict between traditionalism and modernity which has raged without abatement since the *nahda*, or Arab renaissance of the 19th century. From there he goes on to denounce censorship in art and literature, arguing that art is by nature 'subversive', investigative and intrusive, whereas censorship is backward-looking, traditional and sanctifying of the very idols art sets out to smash. Platitudinous as these postulations may sound, they are indicative of the kind of debates that Mahfouz and other intellectuals of the period felt the need to engage in.

One thing the reader misses in reading these collections of Mahfouz's journalism is the beauty of language, the elegance of style, the imagination. It is all very direct, purely communicative and down to earth; nothing of his artistic flair filters into the writing. It is as if he assumed a completely independent persona when he wrote these articles. You look hard for a trace of the great novelist and powerful stylist but you find none. What is amazing is that at the time when he was writing this insipid journalism in the 1970s and 1980s he was also bringing into being some of his most imaginative and ground-breaking works of fiction. Another disappointment in reading these essays is their tendency to diagnose the problem and offer the solution in very simple terms, in essays that consist mostly of two hundred words: cliché solutions for endemic and age-old problems like authoritarian rule and democracy, corruption, religious intolerance, etc. At such moments, one misses the subtle, multi-layered textures of his fiction and somehow wishes he had never stooped to journalism and current affairs.

Mahfouz emerges from these articles, spanning the best part of seven years, as the eternal optimist, or such is the public stance he adopts anyway. He gave Sadat the benefit of the doubt and appeared to take seriously, or pretend to, his so-called Corrective Revolution, or the Revolution of 14 May as it was sometimes called to mark a departure from Nasser's 23 July (1952) Revolution, and later his token restoration of political parties. He also supported his peace initiative with Israel and kept quiet over his increasing dictatorial tendencies in the run up to his assassination. Later he was to show support to his successor too, Mubarak, who took over in 1981, and welcome a new era and a different style of leadership, as it then appeared.

With the benefit of hindsight, it is ironic to read an essay with the title 'Art, Politics and Internationalism' (30/4/1981) written some seven years before Mahfouz was to be awarded the Nobel Prize for Literature.

In the essay he tackles dismissively the debate about whether Arabic literature has achieved an international status. He argues sarcastically that it is not as if Egypt had sorted out all of its cultural and other problems and had nothing to worry about but international recognition. He cites an illiteracy rate of 80 percent in addition to what he calls 'the illiteracy of the educated'. He calls on the nation first to learn to read, watch and listen before aspiring to global glory. Nonetheless, without intending to, he went ahead and achieved internationalism for Arabic literature in 1988 by winning the Nobel Prize.

April 2017

Rasheed El-Enany
Professor of Modern Arabic and Comparative Literature
Doha Institute for Graduate Studies
Professor Emeritus, University of Exeter

Religion and School

Religion is taught as a scientific subject in schools. Their doorways display verses from the Qur'an, sayings of the prophet, articles of faith, and devotions as a matter of course. Pupils memorise these and are tested on them, then they are forgotten, just as others have forgotten what they learned about those subjects which are outside the sphere of their specialisation. Pupils absorb very little of these writings as they stumble between the stylistic eloquence and exact meaning of the words – they endure it because they have to.

Religion is neither a science nor a branch of knowledge; rather, it is a spiritual teaching whose essence becomes manifest through social intercourse, behaviour, and vision. It is often the case that a student who possesses outstanding intelligence will also possess a bad character; he will achieve the highest grade in religion and the baseness of his character may be dismissed! Thus, the student emerges believing that there is no connection between religion and daily living, and how to act in accordance with it.

Because of this, I propose that religious lessons should provide spiritual education. They should provide guidance and be given in an atmosphere of affection and love. Such an approach would mark a significant departure away from the toils of memorising and reciting, along with the fear of lapsing. The idea here is that religion is not something to be memorised, but that it pertains to one's conduct and behaviour, which are the foundations of human decency.

Furthermore, I view the biography of Prophet Muhammad as being the first pillar of this education insofar as it provides a sublime example of living, conduct, and vision. The biography of Muhammad should be taught to pupils in their first year of primary school through to their second year in high school. When they enter into their first year they would be exposed to a shortened, simplified version; subsequently, with each year, this would gradually become more advanced and incorporate greater detail, with verses from the Qur'an being incorporated according to the need and the level of the pupils. Verses pertaining to salat would be introduced at a specified age,[1] as well as those pertaining to the fast during Ramadan. There would be a focus on verses dealing with humanitarian values, morals and goals. Furthermore, the pupils could be assessed in these lessons in light of their behaviour toward their peers, how they interact with their teachers, their attitude towards learning, their opinions with regard to racial and social justice, as well as religious tolerance – there should be no bigotry – and according to their sense of national unity.

With regard to the third year in secondary school, pupils should study from a text book which includes selected passages on the thought of leading Muslim thinkers – as well as other intellectuals who belong to other religions – with regard to Islam, its humanitarian values, and its message in the modern era.

I am of the view that the degree of success that students attain in the subject of 'behaviour' is the measure of success with regard to their religious education overall.

8 June 1974
AB

1 Salat (*al-ṣalāt*) is the obligatory, ritual prayer performed by Muslims five times a day.

The Issue of Platforms

1. Do differing political currents exist amongst our people?

Yes, because the dissolution of the parties only put an end to their *official* activity. As for their existence, as long as the causes for this – difference in opinions and interests – are abundant, there is no way to root them out. Indeed, no one disputes the fact that the conflicting political currents I have referred to exist, such as Marxism, liberalism, and religious ones, in addition to democratic socialism, which represents the revolutions of 1952 and 1971, and whose emblem the Socialist Union raised up.[1]

2. Did these currents find their way into the Socialist Union?

Yes, this became clear with the creation of the proposed platforms. The creation of a leftist platform was proposed; secondly, a religious one; and thirdly, a liberal one, and so forth. Therefore, these currents do exist in the Socialist Union, and they operate within the sphere of the 'coalition of the people's forces' solidifying their own particular domain in accordance with the current circumstances that the Arab nation is experiencing. Furthermore, some believe in the validity of the coalition's form for all time, while some others believe that healthy political

1 Mahfouz here is referring to the 23 July Revolution of 1952 led by Muhammad Naguib and Gamal Abdel Nasser, and the Corrective Revolution of 1971 under Sadat. The 'Socialist Union' refers to the Arab Socialist Union, a political party founded by Gamal Abdel Nasser in 1962.

life requires the establishment of parties, sooner or later, in accordance with the circumstances and conditions.

3. To which camp do you belong?

I belong to the camp in favour of parties, for the following reasons:

- —Without parties it is not democracy, and without parties it is not freedom.
- —Political democracy and social democracy are not in conflict with one another.
- —Parties are actual realities. Thus, the question can be reduced to the following: Do we acknowledge reality, or do we shut our eyes to it?
- —That which befell our party-political life in the past is attributable to colonialism and the throne, not to party politics itself.
- —Despite politics taking hold over our life in the past, considerable social progress has been achieved under its patronage, such as labour laws, the exemption from taxes for farmers with small holdings, the remission of fees for some stages of education, and the establishment of welfare programmes for the disabled and the elderly, just as the foundation for industry was laid under its auspices.
- —In reality, the corruption of our former political life is not attributable to democracy, but to dictatorship. With the exception of a few years, we did not have a democratic, party-political system. For the rest of the time, all of it, we were governed by one individual: either the king or the British ambassador. Thus, the corruption of the past was due to dictatorship and its continuation after 1952 – this would have almost put an end to the revolution itself had it not been for the doses of democracy with which it reinforced itself in the Corrective Revolution.

4. Do you view the founding of parties as a victory?

It will do no harm to begin the platforms experiment.

5. What do you envision with regard to the platforms?

That they will be built upon foundations of reality, i.e., on the political currents existing in the Socialist Union – provided that they do not pursue independent intellectual activity, such as propagating their varying philosophies. Rather, it will be enough for us that their opinion is expressed with regard to the implementation of matters that concern us, such as that of opening up to private investment, the role of the public sector, taxation, education, and so forth.

6. Will this achieve the desired democracy?

Provided that the executive powers abide by the view that wins the confidence of the majority of the Union.

29 November 1975

AB

Virtual Unemployment

Much is being said these days about what is called virtual unemployment, with reference to university graduates who are routinely and automatically allotted civil service or public sector jobs regardless of whether there is any work for them. As a result, both sectors suffer from a glut of employees, with more being added each year, and this has created a dire problem which upsets the system, with the state carrying an enormous and seemingly never-ending burden. It goes without saying that any employee who is superfluous to need within a government administration threatens its smooth running, upsets its operational ability, and there will be ramifications in the public institutions connected with it. The same applies to a superfluous employee in an economic unit, a company or organisation. He upsets its balance sheets, distorts its manpower capacity and ends up being a burden on the public. On the other hand, however, should we abandon our children to unemployment in these trying times? Do we just let our educated elite go to waste during this crippling crisis? It has been suggested that they could be organised into work units without any having to forgo their incomes.

Firstly, any organisation or company must divest itself of those who are surplus to requirements in order to enable us to guarantee the integrity, organisation and system of work.

Secondly, we should transfer those surplus to requirements to augment the workforce of the Ministry of Manpower while guaranteeing their salaries, eligibility for pay rises and associated rights. On this basis, the Ministry of Manpower will become the largest ministry, and perhaps the one with the biggest budget. At that point we will be faced with the following important question: What can we do with all these civil servants? Or to put it more bluntly: What are we to do with all this reserve manpower which just keeps growing and growing?

I imagine that we will be able to deal with this as follows:

1. We should appoint some of them, according to their date of graduation, as civil servants for which the administration has real need.
2. Some of them should be given work in places where people are usually reluctant to go due to the hardship of the work there or the location's remoteness.
3. Those with the requisite qualifications should be given teacher training and we would thereby be able to provide the Ministry of Education with the hundreds of thousands of employees it lacks which it has not been able to recruit for years.
4. A requisite number should be chosen from them to fight illiteracy. Once illiteracy has been eradicated according to a well-defined plan, the funds usually expended on that can be used for other purposes.
5. We should prepare those with the required expertise for work in the Arab states and elsewhere.
6. The remainder should be deemed to be on a sabbatical so that they can achieve higher degrees in science and research and gain new field expertise which will transform them from merely a reserve human workforce into an outstanding group with scientific and cultural expertise. These people would be exportable as well as being of use for translation, writing or general educational service.

This suggestion might provide a solution, even if temporary, to this recalcitrant problem.

2 February 1976

RH

The Scarecrow

The scarecrow is a type of effigy meant to frighten, and I use this as a metaphor for the type of bureaucracy prevalent in an administration but which serves a slightly different role. A scarecrow does not, as in the origin of the word, defend crops from birds, but forms an unassailable barrier for people in search of their rights, and accords them untold misery. However, I believe that it is a semi-imaginary impediment at most; its force inflated by the popular imagination and the fear of it is generated by those cunning enough to exploit its bad reputation for their own ends. In truth, bureaucracy is a collection of laws and regulations and, as such, it needs to be reviewed from time to time, developed and renewed, and empowered to confront the problems of our time, but bureaucracy is not an island unto itself, it is something implemented by civil servants, and if development and reform do not take the power and intellect of these civil servants into account, any new plan will become bogged down and every effort made to implement any desired reforms will end up as naught.

At this point I think it is worth my mentioning a rather ordinary memory I have. I had a job in the Ministry of Religious Endowments, which is proverbial for its complicated bureaucracy. Then the late Abdel Salam al-Shadhli was appointed minister. He was a man known for his decisiveness and force of personality, may he rest in peace. From his very first day in the ministry he ordered the doors of the ministry to be locked at exactly eight o'clock in the morning and that any employees who turned up later would have a day deducted from their holiday allowance in the first instance, and thereafter a day's pay would be deducted from their salary. Very soon the working day started to run like clockwork, with no distinction made between the most senior manager and the lowliest office boy. Then, the minister allowed one door to be opened from nine o'clock, with two clerks posted behind it, one of whom manned an information desk and the other one was from the investigations administration. When someone approached the ministry, he would be asked his purpose. If he was someone coming for a social call he was turned away,[1] and if he was there for official business, the information clerk would contact the specific department and either he would receive the appropriate answer or would be given an appointment. At the appointed time the information clerk would go to the department to be informed about what had transpired. If there were delays, an investigating clerk would follow up and send a memo to the minister, and the smallest sanction for this was that the relevant official would lose two weeks' salary. There was one occasion when a clerk was negligent in sending out rent demands which led to the Ministry losing two hundred pounds in revenues and the minister immediately ordered that the sum should be recouped from the clerk's salary over a period of four years. In those days I used to see high-ranking employees of the Ministry, when they were called in for a meeting with the minister, waiting in front of his door, buttoning up their jackets, muttering invocations to God and whispering Qur'anic verses before being asked to enter. How happy was the man who exited, his face beaming, not having been rebuked or punished, for His Excellency was in the habit of disciplining the high and mighty and not just the lowly.

What happened to the bureaucratic regime in the Ministry during those heady days?

It became a byword for discipline, results, transparency, income generation and productivity. The spectre of bureaucracy disappeared.

---

1 The Egyptian civil service, which offered every graduate a job, was vastly overstaffed and underworked. The reference to someone turning up for a social call symbolises the fact that most civil servants had almost nothing to do but sit around and pass the time idly.

No one heard about it anymore, it was no longer used as an excuse for inaction, and I realised in those days that the essential problem was now only the minister himself or, at the most, the minister and the clerk.

I should like to reiterate: I do not mean by what I have said that bureaucracy is some sort of fairy tale. It is an old established system which is in need of renewal, but I also believe that it wrongs innocent people, it allows cunning people to operate, and that the core of a good solution can be summed up in two words: minister and clerk.

9 February 1976

RH

Millions and Pennies

Government here is a centralising totalitarian power which casts its shadow over our homeland from north to south and from east to west. By dint of its power it controls the economy, just as it controls politics and our daily life. It possesses surveillance apparatus of every type as well as unlimited power. Thus, it has total responsibility and must come to terms with its own power, and it must also forgive people if something pains them or if things go drastically wrong, and for wondering where the government is?

Indeed, there are many types of wrongdoing over which it is impossible to have full control, and dissolution, bribe-taking and embezzlement cannot always be stopped before they take place even if they can then be controlled and limited to the nth degree. The same goes for violence, aggression, kidnapping and pilfering – these are all examples of wrongdoing which can be followed up and treated although not in one fell swoop, particularly in these trying times when pressures fly in from all directions.

However, all these types of wrongdoing almost pale into insignificance when compared to a phenomenon which is the topic of much conversation these days – that of the millionaires created by our society which should actually be moving towards socialism or, let's say, towards social justice. We should not doubt the truth of this phenomenon for the simple reason that the topic has lately been much on the tongues of officials whose good intentions are beyond doubt and who are keenly aware of what people are talking about, not to mention the word on the street. The dangerous aspect of this phenomenon is that it goes beyond the personal domain and has an egregious effect on the fate of the population, on the suffering of the masses and the reputation of the state.

Some people say that all these millions may be the fruit of legitimate work or legitimate gain which is not in contravention of the law and in the making of which there was no exploitation of the labouring masses, but I wonder what sort of legitimate work can produce a profit of millions within a short period of time? If the work was legitimate, and the profit also legitimate, has the correct amount of tax been paid to the state? And if it has been, how can someone amass millions within the purview of the current tax laws?

So I would state that it is beyond doubt that these sort of unimaginable riches can only have been amassed in an illegal, unlawful and illegitimate manner, and are clearly the product of a world of backhanders, smuggling, secret monopolies, and so on.

Another question has been confusing me: Did the people who have uncovered this phenomenon arrive at it through deduction and imagination, by the power of abstract thought and spiritual emanations, or from having seen living examples and physical proof? And if this is the case, then why have they not informed the relevant authorities, even secretly and without evidence, so that they could carry out the requisite enquiries, investigations and arrests?

Another question: Since the matter has been uncovered by some people, why was it not uncovered earlier or even later by the authorities who are tasked with monitoring financial affairs?

The question is not secondary, nor does it convince us to be sympathetic with those caught up in it, but embezzlement on this scale cannot be countenanced in a country which suffers such a budgetary imbalance or dreadful condition as ours. It is a heinous crime against people struggling to earn a crust of bread, who suffer night and day from undernourishment, from preventable diseases, and a lack of public services.

Our need for political parties and pulpits may be less – at this moment at least – than our need for police officers, informers, prisons and gallows.

23 February 1976

RH

The Accusations against Nasser and Freedom of the Press

I was happy to hear what the president said about exculpating the late President Gamal Abdel Nasser from the accusations against him. This is a piece of good news about which every Arab, even his enemies, should be happy. That is because the accusations against Abdel Nasser were not levelled against an individual but against Egypt and nationalist rule which stems from our ability to rule ourselves. The objection of the imperialists, which they used as a pretext to govern us, is that we were incapable of governing ourselves, and that, if we should gain true independence and take over the administration of our own affairs, our claims to be able to govern ourselves would prove hollow and we would ruin ourselves. I have criticised the late leader, but I criticised him, and still do, from a position of being part of the revolution, confirming at the same time his great revolutionary legacy which liberated the peasants just as it liberated the national economy, which was reborn through agriculture and manufacturing, and which flung the door to social justice wide open. The shortcomings I saw in him were those which unfortunately can be found in great people and not those temptations of life which seduce weaker-willed people. That is why I was saddened to see him accused and was overcome with such despondency that only God knows its extent. Then came the good news and my distress and sorrow disappeared. It should also be mentioned that Gamal al-Din al-Hamamsy was not the first to raise these accusations for there had been rumours going around for years, weaving their web of accusations against the leader, with fairy tales about totally fantastic amounts of smuggled money.[1] The gossips picked up on these rumours and so embellished them with purported facts that they appeared to be no more than repeated truths. I used to hear all this and seethe with anger, unable to put a stop to all this rumour-mongering. Perhaps the censorship authorities picked up on these rumours flying around, and perhaps they simply made a note of them and analysed them without responding or investigating. When Gamal al-Din al-Hamamsy started to repeat these in the form of musings in his articles, the authorities moved into action and started a speedy investigation which showed the late leader to have been squeaky clean. Had it not been for the decent actions of a journalist and freedom of the press, these rumours would not have been dissipated and the truth would not have come out, and the reputation of an incorrupt man and that of our dear homeland would not have been exculpated. Let us remember that as we think about the freedom of the press. Let us remember that heinous lies dress themselves up as the truth in the penumbra of oppression, but they meet their inevitable fate, indescribably awful as they may have been, in an atmosphere of freedom and happiness.

22 March 1976
RH

1 Gamal al-Din al-Hamamsy (1913–1988) was a leading journalist.

Imported Ideas

The term 'imported ideas' is on the verge of becoming a curse on thinking, due to long years of criticism and carping. The issue is not about the import or export of ideas but it is, first and foremost, about what humanity needs to support its development towards a form of progress in which there is no difference between ideas and ideologies on the one hand, and investment and consumer goods on the other. From the historical point of view, the import of ideas is a policy that has been followed since time immemorial and is carried out both spontaneously by means of individuals involved in trade and travel, and by the design of enlightened rulers. Thus, civilisation was transported from the ancient East to Greece and thence to Rome, and when the Islamic state established its structure, as well as its developed religious base, it looked to imported concepts. Perhaps this practice of importing first took place during the era of the prophet, and the outstanding example of this can be discerned in the originally-Persian concept of trench digging.[1]

We are importers. In olden times we imported Christianity from Palestine and Islam from the Arabian Peninsula. In modern times, we have imported science, democracy and socialism from Europe. There have always been reactionaries and Luddites who have warned against imported thought, people who tried to close the windows on

1 This is a reference to the famous Battle of the Trench in 627 when, upon the suggestion of Salman the Persian, a trench was dug to defend the city of Medina against an attacking army of non-Muslims.

the world. This does not mean that we should sanctify everything imported, or lose the necessary pragmatism to digest or develop what comes from abroad in order to adapt it to our reality. We also do not need to import frivolous items or concepts, but that is one thing and closing our windows to the world is another thing completely.

It is indeed the grossest mistake to imagine that our cultural authenticity can only be reliant upon our own history or to see anything foreign as a challenge. Cultural authenticity is not the necessary or inevitable result of our heritage and all forms of innovation stem basically from that very freedom of thought in which, by dint of observation and discernment, the old and the new, the domestic and the foreign, find their own level and which accepts or rejects various aspects according to their usefulness following a process during which they are examined and tried out in practical situations. The crucial point for me in determining what constitutes good or progress, is that it should enhance our lives at this point in time, fill a need and help create the requisite justice, freedom and atmosphere of cultural creativity.

Between Fear and Intrusion

This fear of imported ideas is odd at a time when the world's nations are closer together than at any time previously. In our time, the whole world has been discovered, and there are good political, economic and cultural relations between its farthest-flung reaches. Movement from one side of the world to the other has become easier and quicker than journeying from one country to the next in the ancient world. Anything that occurs in one place has reverberations everywhere else, and the discovery of minerals in the ground, or a coup d'état somewhere, is followed by shockwaves in the greatest and most powerful centres of civilisation. As we stride towards world unity, we must contribute the requisite amount of talent to this symphony in order to play together in tune and prevent the musical output from slipping into disharmony or cacophony, for life will continue to be an untrammelled and continuous process which knows no stopping or recoiling no matter what mistakes or relapses it has been subjected to, whatever myriad crises have attempted to mute it. That is why the dream of a paradise lost in the mists of time seems to be a puerile stance, with all its paramount fear about today and tomorrow symbolising a lack of self-confidence and an attempt to flee from responsibility and ideas with the result that everything becomes worthless. The role of our heritage in this battleground is none other than to provide a shining exemplar of an unrepeatable and unique success, and to be a value with which to nurture people so that they can seek out ever new fields which accord with the eternal flow of life in which reactionary forces also have a role and which can also be a lesson for us. These reactionary forces may well be fighting a losing battle, but their obstinacy makes us think again and teaches us to avoid recklessness. Even though these reactionary forces are generally on the losing side, they perform an unintended purpose. It can thus be said that that those pushing the wheel forwards, as well as those trying to hold it back, participate in progress.

Subversive Art

That leads us anew to the topic of censorship and art. Censorship has long been onerous, as the poet Sharif Razi said:[2]

You are the happiness of my heart and its torture
My heart lives for your command and your sweetness.
I have messages of love I do not remember
But for the censor, I would have conveyed them to your mouth.

Except that enlightened censorship means monitoring art and not censoring it. Its starting point must be one of love and appreciation; it should be always ready to come to an understanding with art without arbitrariness or intransigence and bring to it a gentle awareness of the unintended hyperbole or aberrations which only appeal to the spirit

2 A Shia scholar and poet (970–1015), best known for *The Peak of Eloquence (Nahj al-balāgha),* a compilation of the sermons, precepts, prayers, epistles and aphorisms of Imam Ali.

of commercialism or cheap success. In its essence, proper censorship should be more akin to criticism and only prevent art from giving its message when created by those unfit for purpose.

However, there is another type of censorship which generally stems from undervaluing art, artists and progress, whose starting point is wariness, contempt and hatred and whose only aim is to make art subservient to its 'parents' – the state and society which bestow it with a conservative content, nay a highly conservative content, waving scissors about in one hand and a stick in the other, wrapped up in their regulations and narrow mindedness, as if the cure is to be found in the debasement and shackling of the human spirit, and which exert themselves to instil inflexibility and offer death.

Art is a rebellious youth spurred into action by contradictions and by the hissing sound of negativity, who then rolls up his sleeves and sets to work against all the criticism and intrusiveness of the state by elegising all manner of things and announcing the new and the strange, by complying with the dynamic and innovative stream of life which flows with full force towards an unknown tomorrow.

Censorship lashes this rebellious youth to the status quo, directs his attention to the past, and, while he dreams of latent revolutions, it bids him to sanctify worn-out traditions and moribund customs just as he is about to smash the idols and set fire to outmoded means of expression. Just as one cannot avoid seeing the ridiculous, there is an inevitability about this clash. For that reason, there can be no peace or agreement between the censor and the rebellious youth until one has vanquished the other, and so we end up with either strong censorship and no art, or art without censorship. I worked as the general director of censorship at the Bureau of Arts in 1959, and I used to tell my colleagues 'Creativity in the written word lies in open-mindedness and any slight against it should be considered, like divorce, to be the most hateful thing in the eyes of God.'

The Ethics of Society and the Ethics of the Screen

This leads us on to draw a comparison between what takes place in society and what can be seen on the large and small screen. It is well known that the cinema in some Western countries has an astonishing freedom to depict sex that we might consider here ugly and disgusting, but it is paralleled by a similar sexual freedom in society to the extent that sexual deviation is protected and guaranteed by law. As for our society, we still sanctify traditional ethics and spiritual values. In spite of that, we have factories producing wine and we allow advertisements encouraging people to drink. We open casinos in our tourist resorts and our parks witness unusual sights which we tolerate. We speak of what takes place on al-Haram Street with no embarrassment.[3] Our summer resorts have become places of exhibition for half-naked bodies, and we see nothing the matter with that for perhaps we see them as landmarks of beauty and civilisation. Some people may consider this outrageous and some may see it as a sign of development, for to each his own outlook on life. In any case, if a nation condemns what is taking place as decadence and sets about trying to change it, they will have to declare holy war on society in bars, casinos, brothels and other places of easy morals. However, we do not expect them to declare war on the cinema and the television as if they offer a reality which society reflects, as society is the reality and the screen is merely its reflection. It is impossible for immorality to appear on the screen without it being a reflection of a social reality. It does not appear on the screen for the purpose of titillation but the artist depicts it because merely showing it on screen shows up its ugliness and the role it plays in the destruction of the human spirit. It is as if it is not enough for us just to ignore what is taking place in our society, but we also insist on shackling those who use artistic means to highlight immorality.

Furthermore, there is no point in laying siege to art in order to artificially clean up what appears on the screen. Should we not instead direct our weapons towards the real evil which is besetting society?

10 May 1976

RH

3 Al-Haram Street is broad avenue in Giza known for its 'oriental' nightclubs.

Arabs and Civilisation

In the magazine *Arab Horizons* the translator writes about a secret document from 1902[1] in which Campbell-Bannerman,[2] the British prime minister, says of our Arab East that 'There are people who control spacious territories teeming with manifest and hidden resources. They dominate the intersections of world routes. Their lands were the cradles of human civilizations and religions. These people have one faith, one language, one history and the same aspirations. No natural barriers can isolate these people from one another … if, perchance, this nation were to be unified into one state, it would then take the fate of the world into its hands and would separate Europe from the rest of the world. Taking these considerations seriously, a foreign body should be planted in the heart of this nation to prevent the convergence of its wings in such a way that it could exhaust its powers in never-ending wars. It could also serve as a springboard for the West to gain its coveted objects.'

We do not need a secret report to remind us of the battle for Arab unity or its decisive consequences for creating a strong nation or a world force. That is why millions of Arabs are so vociferous about it – not in order to hive Europe off from the rest of the world or to dominate the fate of the world, but to achieve the aim of self-determination

1 The report was dated 1907 and was intended to be presented at the Colonial Conference of 1907 (later called the Imperial Conference).

2 Sir Henry Campbell-Bannerman (1836–1908), prime minister 1905–1908.

among the nations of the world and to contribute elements from their glorious past and the bloody efforts of modern times to the ebb and flow of world culture. However, we should not cease recalling that our enemy keeps trying to shatter our power in continuous wars. Oddly, our enemy's scheming against us is not sufficient so we help him to realise his goals with our own ceaseless disarray and by so exhausting our own forces in regional disputes that we have all become despondent and can no longer believe in Arab unity.

I am left wondering when people's hearts and minds will realise that they should not wish for that, particularly now as they face an arrogant enemy ever ready to launch a murderous and treacherous war, and I wonder also whether now is the right time for Algeria and Morocco to be exchanging fire, for Arabs to be fighting each other in Lebanon, or for Egypt, Syria and Lebanon to be feuding.

The most wondrous thing is that we have the Arab League, an institution which over time has now built up a history and traditions of its own. The League should have been able to resolve any dispute, or to have been able to contain intractable differences until it could come up with civilised and respectable short-term or long-term solutions. However, we have allowed the Arab League, as the foremost symbol of our unity and the preordained hope for our future, to crumble and disintegrate. Unity is still far off, but the League is still operating. We have to make it the foundation stone of the edifice we wish for but that will only come about when we strengthen the League and grant it freedom of operation. We have to make it the sanctuary where the Arabs can come together over what they agree about firstly, and then over how they can handle their differences. And what they agree about, or may agree about, is important, risky and replete with ramifications for our present and our future. In that regard I should like to mention the topic of economic and cultural integration by way of example as perhaps that is what will provide real support for any future political union.

Our greatest need may be the convening of a summit conference to outline the future shape of the Arab nation which will include studying how to grant more power to the Arab League, including active power, and drawing up a meaningful Arab plan for cultural and economic development aimed at creating a modern, educated and spiritual Arab nation and at setting up an authority charged with planning and implementation.

This is a cultural and historical duty, and we have the means of success such as material, manpower and spiritual resources. Thereafter complacency will be seen as unforgivable treachery.

The State of the Arabs Today

The Arabs occupy a great part of the earth and number more than 140 million, but their industrial productivity is only half a percent of total world output, and their agricultural output represents even less than that. Three quarters of the Arabs are illiterate, and their scientific level has not yet reached a level which allows them to participate in innovation on an international level. This is something about which we cannot be silent or patient any longer, and dribs and drabs of individual endeavour are not enough to extricate us from this situation. Experts have estimated that if the developing countries are left to their own devices in terms of economic and cultural development, it will take another two hundred years for the Arabs to reach the level of the advanced nations, but in the meantime what other achievements will the advanced nations have made? Will this alarming gap among the peoples of the earth continue forever? What we have to fear most is that during that period some people will have acquired such superior capabilities that we will be left in a permanent state of serfdom or extinction.

However, there is the gift which fate has bestowed upon the Arabs, i.e., oil – a special privilege not granted to any other developing nation. Oil does not create civilisations or innovate science, but this gift has brought a huge inflow of funds which, if prudently applied, can create miracles and has the exceptional ability to help the Arabs catch up with advanced nations. Hence, oil is not merely a mineral wealth but a test and a mission. In the past the Arabs came out of the desert and established a global culture thanks to Islam, and today they have been called upon to bring their civilisation into the modern age thanks to oil – and not to do so would be a betrayal of history, religion and the modern age. It is undeniable that they have handed out aid and made investments, but the matter still needs two fundamental elements:

1. A comprehensive plan for all the Arab states, drawn up with the participation of all Arab experts and some foreign consultants with the aim of reclaiming every inch of land, reviving manufacturing in all its spheres, and setting up scientific and cultural research centres. That is how they will bring modern activity to the Arab homeland and how the oil-producing countries will guarantee or even double their resources before energy reserves run out.
2. A robust belief in ourselves as a driving force for action, with us being reliant upon our eternal spiritual, Islamic and Christian values, so that we can savour some of the progress of the developed nations and benefit from the establishment of social justice.

The Arab leaders should try and outdo each other to achieve this aim instead of squabbling and vying over vanities.

Will We Die Out like the Dinosaurs?

There has been global news about inclement weather which will last for forty years, threatening to bring calamity to the agricultural yields necessary for human life. There are also some predictions that a nuclear bomb might be used as an unavoidable means of guaranteeing a food supply. Even before this period of inclement weather starts, millions of humans are suffering from hunger on an ongoing basis, and from famine from time to time. The aggravated problem of world overcrowding being permanently out of control will bring humanity to a state of crisis whether the weather becomes worse or not, and if science does not save the situation with some miracle or other, mankind will be like a sinking ship with the captain only having a limited number of lifeboats. Do not think that this is purely a figment of the imagination, for how many species have died out, as if they never existed or had nothing more than an ephemeral existence? Among these were not only the dinosaurs who ruled the earth but more than one species of *homo erectus* has also disappeared, such as Java Man, Peking Man and others, and they only differed from modern man in the size of their brain and some facial features. After careful selection, and out of fear of non-existence, only the fittest will live on, that is those who are advanced in the modern meaning of the word.

Thus, either we establish a flourishing infrastructure in our countries before the oil wells run dry, or we will face non-existence.

The Conscience of the World

Some people cannot imagine that such dreadful events can come to pass, but anything can actually happen. What we call 'the conscience of the world' is a new concept for which the League of Nations established a temple on earth, but that temple is still shaky, particularly when compared with our national conscience which is still lamenting the Denshawai Incident,[3] Badrashin,[4] and Deir Yassin.[5] When it comes to the conscience of the world, however, these distressing incidents hardly make a dent. I have been following the news of the earthquake in Italy and am amazed to see that it may have left a mark on people's

3 The Denshawai Incident took place in 1906. A scuffle broke out between some British officers and Egyptian peasants in the Nile Delta. After a summary trial, some of the peasants were sentenced to death, some to imprisonment and some were flogged in front of their families. The incident is seen by Egyptian nationalists as an important turning point in the British occupation of Egypt.

4 An incident when British soldiers killed and defiled the women of Badrashin. Mahfouz included an account of this incident in his 1965 novel *Palace Walk* (*Bayn al-Qaṣrayn*).

5 This is a reference to the 1948 massacre by the Zionist paramilitary groups Irgun and Lehi of over 100 Palestinians at the village of Deir Yassin during the conflict which led to the emergence of the state of Israel.

memory as we read and hear about it with a sense of indifference.[6] We seem to have lost our emotions and imagination. I think that the explanation for that is the amount of continuous coverage given to world events in the media. The daily newspapers, from their first page to the death notices, are full of natural, political and economic catastrophes and only rarely does some news item make us smile or feel optimistic. That is the job of the advertisements. By dint of their daily frequency, we have become complacent about catastrophes. They come across as regular news items. That is how we have lived through the massacres of the Great War,[7] the Vietnam War, the rape of Palestine, the earthquakes in Yugoslavia and Italy, and how we paid scant attention to the greatest crime in human history which was the dropping of atom bombs on Hiroshima and Nagasaki. We read about these distressing events and we are hardly affected by them as they have become daily events in the modern media and we suffer from disaster fatigue. That is how all sorts of catastrophes can take place without having any effect on world conscience except for a fear of their repercussions. We defended our right with logic and an appeal to values, but no one listened to us. Then we waged the October War and oil was used as a weapon, and we found that people everywhere listened to us. And I will finish by restating: either we establish a flourishing infrastructure in our countries before the oil runs out, or we will be exposing ourselves to non-existence.

24 May 1976
RH

6 Known as the Terremoto del Friuli, the earthquake struck northeast Italy on 6 May 1976.

7 He says the Great War, but one would assume he means World War II.

Poor and Noble

Every epoch has a philosophy appropriate for it, and by philosophy I mean a way of seeing and behaving. In this definition, every individual has his own philosophy inspired by the circumstances of his environment and the conditions of his life. Perhaps the best description that can be applied to us today is that we are constructivists, because at every moment we are being called upon to renovate, renew, establish and build more and more, hoping thereby to assure our place in history. Our slogan should be 'give it some elbow grease', more effort in war, more effort in peace, more effort for oneself and, hence, the philosophy of our time should be based on austerity and work.

The state has started implementing austerity, saving millions of pounds from its budget and demanding that this should continue until every last penny has been saved, but it is nonsensical to ask for aid or loans when every last penny has already been accounted for.

Three quarters of the population are already living in a state of austerity and do not wish to see it made even more acute. When it comes to the other quarter of the population, they have not evinced any readiness to make any serious sacrifices. There is an outflow of millions of pounds every year to pay for the import of lifestyle items such as cars, luxury food and innumerable other accessories, all of which they could forego out of a sense of identification with the people and as part of a greater national salvation plan.

We do not wish to see encroachments on the rights of the citizen but we would like to see more weight given to education, culture, employment, health, freedom, dignity and communications inter alia. Much of what is being spent on food, clothing and housing could, particularly in these days, be spent on health, public hygiene and welfare rather than on ostentation and luxury items. In fact, all this frivolity can only lead to an impasse and all this never-ending search for fun can only be detrimental to bodily and spiritual health as people give themselves over to a search for ever more pleasures and fancies. Unfortunately this wisdom has been long diluted by a stream of Egyptian films which have aimed at keeping the poor happy in their poverty, and by the statements of some people who do not accept the accusation that they are drowning in frivolity. However, that does not stop it being real wisdom or common sense, and our duty today is perceived by everyone except by the lowliest egotists whom the state should stop pampering at the expense of the country.

Recently I read about a French firm which is building an international hotel in Moscow which stipulated that it should be allowed to import food for its employees from France, leading people to sneer about the standard of living in the Soviet Union. It is beyond doubt that there is decent food in Russia, but it appears that it is limited to the bare essentials, and were that not the case it might not have had capability to build its industrial and scientific infrastructure, realise social justice, make progress in the conquest of space, or within half a century bring about a rebirth[1] which took Europe three centuries – without recourse to imperialism or the exploitation of the masses.

What I am demanding is a national duty and a moral, Islamic, political and socialist virtue without which we will all end up the victims of our own gluttony.

Beware of a Bad Reputation

A storm has broken out in parliament about 'senior experts' and

1 Rebirth, here and throughout, is a translation of the Arabic *nahḍa*, which has rather larger overtones and is inspired by the European concept of the Renaissance. Although Arab nationalists used the word nahḍa to mean 'a renaissance', it is felt that 'rebirth' is less misleading to the Western reader.

consultation work taken on by those in cabinet positions and above, who are currently working on cattle husbandry, chicken farming, and imports and exports, with the air having become replete with accusations and theories without any names being mentioned. We do not seem to give a whit about what effect this can have abroad, for the world is full of scandals and our worries about our reputation should not be used to silence criticism, except that a group of degenerates have used this reticence to whistle-blow as their golden opportunity to carry on with their corrupt activities in an atmosphere of peace and security. So, while we do not give a whit about the effect criticism can have abroad, we really do care about the domestic effect when accusations fly around and are not followed up by the requisite inquiries or investigations. The fact that no names are mentioned only serves to broaden the circle of accusations and harms many innocent people. People's imaginations are running riot and striking out at everything arbitrarily at a time when conditions are so difficult that they do not have the energy to show tolerance towards anything that touches their daily life struggle. It can be said that a job in and of itself cannot be considered a bad thing and why should the former minister, or deputy prime minister, not take on some work, provided it is in the service of the state, for it can be seen as a form of public service. However, what raises suspicion is when someone in a position of power uses his position or his former experience at tax evasion, for example, who acquires privileges to which he is not entitled, or exploits his authority in any way at all, for that is the point at which his job goes from being legitimate to criminal activity and we can then ask ourselves whether that is having some effect on our current troubles in the areas of subsidised food supplies and prices, etc. Therefore, I believe that we must be apprised of the names involved and the appropriateness and legality of these jobs, and we must be reassured that the correct tax is being levied. This information should all be made public by the prime minister as he is the person who can give the nation some assurance in these matters.

14 June 1976

RH

Killing Your Brother whether He Is a Criminal or a Victim

If you fall into a trap without knowing that it is a trap, then that is witless and disorganised bad luck, for a clever person is responsible for everything, even the unknown. But what would we call a person who falls into a trap when he knows that it is a trap and has seen someone setting it for him? That is the state of the Arab nations without any exaggeration or evil intention. They know full well that their strength lies in unity and they know full well that their enemy constantly tries to drive a wedge between them, aiming to extend the period of no peace no war as much as possible, and to so overburden us with despair that we will accept any deal imposed on us. On top of that, they also try to deprive our historic victory of any content. Over the last two years we have read about their aims and dreams in that regard, and yet here we are acting out what their imagination has created for us, and here we are fighting with each other mercilessly and tearing each other to shreds unconcernedly. Our victims in their scores, in their hundreds and in their thousands, are paying the price of extremism, obstinacy and short-sightedness.

Do not say that we have many enemies, do not say that we are a toy in the hands of the more powerful states and powers, do not speak about intrigues and intriguers, schemes and schemers, but think, and think deeply, about what is lacking at home, about your own weak points which have made you an easy target for any marksman and a tool for any schemer. Think about that spot within yourselves which should provide illumination and insight but which at the moment exudes no more than precipitateness, nervousness and selfishness.

All that is happening while we are in a state of war, with our territory occupied as we attempt to overcome backwardness, poverty and ignorance, with our enemy attempting to put obstacles in the way of our fate with one hand, and with the other the enemy receives aid and supplies. It is really regrettable, and embarrassing, that we know everything about the trap and can see out of the corner of our eye who has set it for us but then the force of blind anger impels us to fall headfirst into it.

I honestly do not like seeing Egypt a party to any Arab conflict and I would really like to see it preserve its position as the older brother of the Arab nations and to restrict itself to mediating and reconciling the disputing parties. In that connection I would call upon Egypt to show infinite wisdom and endless self-restraint and to gird itself with patience in the face of stupidity, with diplomacy in the face of idiocy, and with forbearing when it comes to adversity and accusations. Egypt should not take its eye off the enemy and its ruses; it should thwart its schemes and tricks, and foil its aims. It should avoid becoming incensed even if that is justifiable. It should refuse to be stirred into action even if that is just and reasonable. Before Egypt makes any public statement or action, it should have a full understanding of the ramifications for Egypt, for Arab nationalism, for the particular case in question and for the third world as well as for the whole world. That is the duty of any politician in this world which has become one large global village.

When Words Lose Their Meaning

Words lose their meaning when used in intentional or unintentional rhetoric: 'this is a genocidal battle with thousands of bombs and thousands of victims', or 'this man is an agent', and 'this state is operating as part of a colonialist Zionist plan'.

In rhetoric words lose their inherent meaning as well as their trust and respect, a crime comes across as less serious and its risks appear insignificant to the extent that if a crime actually does take place it comes across as just another event in our daily life.

If we were to believe what is being said about the war in Lebanon, we would have to agree to the removal of all Palestinians from Lebanon, and if we were to believe that Syria is acting in collaboration with Zionism and colonialism, then how could we allow it to remain a member of the Arab League and how could we meet its prime minister in the Arabian peninsula?[1]

Surely Syria, our brother in arms, has the right to have its officials convey to us its opinion on the matter. Where are the traditions of the Arab League, and where are our duties to Arab nationalism?

Let it be clearly understood here that I am not defending Syria, but, on the other hand, if I am not aware of the opinion of a party to a dispute I cannot know whether to support or oppose him.

It can never be enough for us simply to read the opinions and commentaries that appear in our press, for Syria is not Israel. It is a member of the Arab League and our partner in sacrifice and peace. Syria has been one of the flagships of Arabism over history and has only taken a stance against us since the disengagement agreement.[2] Perhaps Syria is not in the right. Perhaps Syria is actually acting in error, but it does not thereby forfeit its history and its efforts do not become as nought. We should not be prevented from hearing Syria's opinion, so that we can decide, after careful deliberation, whether to be in favour of, or against, its stance and so that this can be the consensus of all the Arab states – for consensus will not only allow Egypt to play its historical role in constructing Arab nationalism and to steer a safe path through troubled waters, but also to do something more important than that which is to work for the economic and cultural integration of the Arab states and to revive their culture on a firm, spiritual basis which may represent our salvation and that of the whole world.

Where is the Arab League?

Unfortunately the Arab League does not occupy the place in the hearts

1 This is a reference to summit meetings held in Saudi Arabia.

2 The Second Egyptian-Israeli Disengagement Agreement, June 1975–March 1976.

of people that it ought to. Its work is bureaucratic rather than forceful. It does not go into action until events spur it on and then only makes symbolic gestures with no real weight to them. In order for it to be the Arab League in name and deed, it must be proactive and not just reactive. Since the Lebanese crisis of 1958,[3] it should have carried out field work, convened conferences, offered solutions or requested officials to make suggestions on its behalf, and its real task in Lebanon should have been averting clashes and crisis management. Its role should have been more than that of an observer or providing lip service to its ideals.

In the same way, the Sahara problem should not have been a surprise to the West.[4] It had long threatened to flare up and the Arab League should really have been involved much earlier. It should have studied the various views and exerted some serious efforts to bring the parties together. It is highly regrettable that the Arab League did not get involved much earlier and simply reacted to events.

Why does the Arab League not have a list of Arab issues covering areas from the East to the West? Why does it not work to resolve them with all its authority and power? Even if it has not managed to resolve them, it is well within its capability to present facts which can spur the conscience of Arab thinkers into action – and, in fact, in that regard it should convene conferences at all levels, by which it will make all Arabs think of it as their own League, accord it the requisite trust, and, on the other hand, be able to play its historic role in the Arab East. It may be that I long to see the Arab League extend its activities from this high political level to evincing an interest in the average Arab individual, in his level of living, his income, his health, his work and his culture, and to come up with suggestions in these domains, meaning that it should be an active intermediary between the Arab countries in the fields of expertise, employment and investment with the aim of narrowing the gap between the life of the man in the street and his hopes, improving

---

3 That is, when American forces intervened militarily in Lebanon to prevent the government being too heavily pro-Egyptian.

4 This 'Sahara problem' is a reference to the Western Sahara becoming a disputed territory following Spain's withdrawal.

its public relations efforts regarding the work it carries out, for at the moment these efforts deal with Arab thought, Arab dreams and Arab culture, and implanting this into the Arab consciousness in a way that it can become a motivating force for the masses and consequently for the various Arab governments.

The Revolution and the Current Situation

The revolution challenges the current situation in order to go beyond it, but not every reality can be challenged. A revolutionary challenges force even if it is immeasurably greater than him, but he cannot ignore the laws of nature, such as gravity. I mention this as I am thinking about the permanent axes of dispute by which I mean the Palestinian resistance or the Palestinian revolution.

This is a true revolution which has emerged from a clamorous string of events as an astonishing reaction to Zionism. Among the things the Palestinian revolution has proved is the value of Arab mineral reserves, and that it is still by far the leading actor and can provide untold examples of self-sacrifice and devotion to a cause. Nothing I say can do even partial justice to the resistance, but I do believe that the time has come for its leaders to review their position in the light of the difficult current circumstances.

I am speaking directly to the members of the resistance when I say that you have great revolutionaries and dedicated fighters amongst you, but, most unfortunately, you do not have a country the way most revolutionaries do. In place of your lost country, you have a welcoming and fraternal homeland for your revolution,[5] but what have the consequences of this been? They have been what took place yesterday in Jordan and what is taking place in Lebanon today. You had problems with your Arab brothers just as you have problems with the Maronites.[6] If extremism is not the motivating factor for the Maronites to turn against you then how can we explain the behaviour of the

5 That is, the 'Arab nation'.

6 The Maronites represent the largest Christian community in Lebanon.

Hashemites?[7] The truth is that a state within a state is not acceptable. Do you think we like seeing your blood shed at the hands of Arabs, or that Arab victims should greatly outnumber Israeli victims? You really have to revise your whole stance.

What do you want? What is possible? What is it that is impossible today but which might become possible in the near or distant future? People gain victory through wisdom as much as they gain victory through revolution.

21 June 1976

RH

7 The Hashemites here refers to the ruling family of Jordan.

Thoughts and Things

During his life a man deals with the thoughts and material items which he experiences, from which he is composed. These are what motivate him, if we were to analyse his motivation, and they are his aims if we single them out. Thoughts include ideologies, religions, philosophy, science and art, and material items are represented by machines and consumer goods inter alia, and normal life requires a balance between these two, between thoughts and things, or between the spirit and materialism as the ancients and those of our times who share the same view have expressed it. Except that there is not always a balance, as thought perhaps gains precedence when civilisation arises, and material items come to the fore as civilisation nears its end. We doubtless all remember what was termed at the time the youth revolution in the West and the explanation for it, or the explanation given by some of the participants that it was a revolution directed against consumerism, against the things which enslave humanity and choke its spirit. Young people declared their rejection of that as a symbol of their return to the visceral and vital elements of life.

There are revolutions and coups d'état in our developing or poor world also. They have been directed against colonialism and poverty but the revolutionaries dreamed of a world of plenty and a world of material things too! Materialism is at the core of two worlds – in the one material goods represent a terrifying nightmare just as they represent a sweet dream for the other. Christianity despises materialism, and urges its followers to pure spirituality, whereas Islam sees no harm in a man taking his portion of material items, but it urges him to give priority to his spiritual life.

Christian Europe has provided the explanation that has enabled it to immerse itself so deeply in materiality that it has achieved the greatest material successes known to history, but now we have its youth pointing out that giving oneself over lock, stock, and barrel to materialism is, in the end, a sad form of revenge and distracts the youth from culture, even its illuminating aspects. Man, as the manufacturer of material items and a consumer is a symbol of strength, domination and wealth, and as the innovator and consumer of thought he is the symbol of man as man, of the sublime and of creation. Thought and the ideology, science and art which stem from it, are the true domain of humanity which brings about honour, happiness and immortality for man. The path of materialism is, at the end of the day, a dead end, and no matter how skilled an individual may be at manufacturing food, his ability to consume it is limited. The same goes for drink and woman; only a few items can provide him with ease, health and beauty, and neither the frantic and hellish fight to acquire wealth, nor the effort he expends doing that, can keep him away from moral turpitude, the wicked exploitation of others, or abjuring his social and national duties. You may have become aware that in this lecture I am addressing a shortcoming which in this period of our life represents a heavy burden on society, and particularly since Egypt has not managed to be a manufacturer of consumer items, but has continued to import and consume them which is the worst possible situation. We need every penny in order to turn the desert into fertile land, to establish factories and research centres, to publish science, culture and art, and to prepare ourselves to look after the millions who will be in their seventies at the end of this century. The model form of life which I advocate at this time, and always, is one in which man is satisfied with the bare material necessities of life and in which he devotes his energies to the worlds of thought and the spirit.

19 July 1976

RH

Islam and the Battle of Ideologies

Competition is heating up among the ideologies inasmuch as they are similar to one another in terms of means and ends. This is where the sense of competition between Islam and Western democracy came from on the one hand, and between Islam and communism on the other. Western democracy is a complete doctrine which has been perfected through theory and application. This doctrine recognises human rights, the free market economy, and has achieved outstanding progress. Communism, likewise, is a complete doctrine; it possesses its own philosophy, economy, and style of governance. It has internationalist aspirations and seeks complete equality among people whether they are white, brown, black or yellow. Communism has also achieved outstanding progress. Islam, however, stands between these two as a contender still trying to open its eyelids after a long, deep slumber in the darkness of apathy and backwardness. Islam certainly senses its backwardness with regard to the advances of modern civilisation in science, technology, and military power. At the same time, however, it has a sense of its past glory and exalted heritage, and this compounds its current crisis, compelling it to think tirelessly in order to make up for what it has lost, and to regain that which has slipped away, so that its essence can then become actualised in accordance with its message.

But perhaps it will not find itself entirely incompatible with Western democracy, even if its own economic model differs from that of the capitalist one. However, Western democracy does not exclude religion, and it is possible to equate its political freedom with the principle of shura.[1] As for the great crime of Western democracy – i.e., colonialism – it has been settled, or almost. And with regard to the sensitivities about the imitation of Western civilisation and the demand for the purity of one's origin, under no circumstances is this a problem that calls for swords to be drawn in revolt against the powers that be – and the same is true with regard to communism.

Communism is a serious matter that cannot be ignored; it has spread over half of the Earth and has plucked individuals and groups from Islam's embrace. It spreads through its propagation of justice and equality among the people in spite of its style of governance and well-known philosophy. So how are leading Muslims to act in the face of this threat? So far they have done nothing more than level accusations, incite the authorities, and make pointless proposals during superficial discussions. Were such actions truly to be considered glorious, then democracy would not have been built, no nation would have gained independence, freedom would not have triumphed anywhere, and the message of Christianity and Islam would not have been actualised formerly. I see no need to demonstrate that intimidation, accusation, and superficiality are futile means for resisting ideologies; rather, ideologies are substantiated by their own particular merit and according to how they benefit the people.

Let's go back a few steps and ask: Why did Islam spread as it did? Islam brought benefits for humanity that had not been combined together in a single doctrine before:

1. It gave the individual a dignified sense of freedom and holiness. It made him caliph of God on Earth, and the angels were commanded by God to bow down before him.
2. It provided comprehensive social justice for the community. It does not combat individual activity but combats poverty and need; it does not permit the existence of these two things within the Muslim community.

---

1 Shura (*al-shūrā*) means 'consultation', or 'counsel', especially in the context of governance and the affairs of state.

3. It ordered man to work and to build, to attain knowledge and wisdom.
4. It respected other faiths; in the public spaces of the Muslim world, Jew and Christian worked side by side with the Muslim in freedom, dignity, and equality. It brought new humane principles into existence with regard to peace, war, and international relations. I do not want to give an in-depth examination or provide a comprehensive presentation, but I do want to affirm that, in its territories, Islam was considered at that time to be an advanced creed, or a progressive one, because of its humaneness – more so than the creeds which prevailed in Persia or Byzantium. In this lies the underlying reason of why it was embraced and why it subsequently spread. This does not mean, in my opinion, that Islam lends itself to all eras and places; however, it is capable – always and forever – of occupying the seat of precedence over other doctrines in any place and in any era. Furthermore, with hard work, it can make up for the time lost during its era of decline and darkness. Islam must examine itself objectively in comparison to other doctrines of governance and politics in order to perceive its shortcomings. There is nothing else for it to do but carry this out so that it can succeed in fully convincing the hearts of contemporary men and women. Furthermore, Islam must provide the same freedom accorded to the individual by Western-style democracy, or more. It must ensure an atmosphere of tolerance and love toward those whose views are contrary to Islam. It must be a faith which provides something better than that which is already available to them in terms of any other given doctrine. In this way – and only in this way – will Islam become a paradise from which none of its adherents will have any desire to leave, for any reason whatsoever; moreover, it will become a centre of attraction for yet others. As for the outcry among young people, the fabrication of charges, and the incitement of the police, these are futile means which were not helpful in the past, and will neither be helpful today nor in

the future. The task is an enormous one; it requires true believers and scholars with expertise who are both bold and diligent, contemporary and innovative, who, at this critical hour, are dedicated, to serving the world and religion.

26 July 1976

AB

O God!

O God, the most gracious! O possessor of glory and munificence! O God, urge the Arabs forth towards civilisation, just as Satan urged them to take up weapons to kill one another and to plot against one another. O God, giver of gifts and blessings, inspire the people of Lebanon to work for the good of their country, just as Satan inspired them to commit acts that served the good of Israel. O God, possessor of guidance and counsel, persuade the Arabs to invest their money in Arab countries rather than investing it in the colonialist countries. O God, the most merciful, inspire our government officials with the ethics of religion and let their hearts know the bitter taste of routine in service to our poor people, O sower of resolution in the hearts of men. O God, assist those who are determined and honest in the fight against neglect – for time has been frittered away with the blowing up of gas pipelines, the burning down of factories, and the poisoning of innocent peasants – assist them to push past the limitations and awaken the consciences. O God, aid the honest and determined to root out corruption so that we see no repeat of the tricks in the Department of Religious Endowments and the Cooperative Agricultural Union, remind them of your great flood, O inflictor of great punishment.[1] O God, deliver us from the irresponsible; they are corrupt and profit from corruption, then they disappear from sight, far from observers, and then [cynically] complain amidst the

1 This, presumably, is a reference to the Genesis flood narrative of the Bible, elements of which are also referred to in the Qur'an.

[genuine] complainants, but you are all-knowing.[2] O God, the most kind, lighten the load of your servants during their overcrowded daily lives, whether when making a journey on public transport or when queuing to buy their groceries. O God, possessor of divine justice, make our elections free and the speech from our minbars honest, and make our democracy clean and strong.[3] O God, strengthen your hold over those who steal jewels and over those from whom jewels have been stolen – and these jewels we alternate among the people.[4] O God of mankind, I seek refuge in you from the retreating whisperer – who whispers in the breasts of mankind – from among the jinn and mankind.[5] O God, if you have recorded me in the Mother Book as neglectful,[6] or corrupt, or exploitative, or as a hypocrite, then annihilate me utterly and scatter me to the winds, O giver of faith and success.

The Seal of the Prophets

Iqbal, the Islamic intellectual and poet, was a proponent of the doctrine that Muhammad – peace be upon him – is the Seal of the Prophets.[7] He said:

---

2 The bracketed words have been inserted for sense. See Mahfouz, Naguib, *Ḥawla l-Dīn wa-l-Dīmūqrāṭīya*, Cairo, 1990, p. 23

3 A minbar (*minbar*) is an elevated platform in a mosque from which the sermon is delivered, similar to a pulpit.

4 Here Mahfouz seems to have adapted an extract from a verse in the Qur'an: 'And these days [of varying conditions] we alternate among the people' (3:140). Mahfouz, however, has replaced 'days' (*al-ayyām*) with 'jewels' (*al-jawāhir*). See Mahfouz, *Ḥawla l-Dīn wa-l-Dīmūqrāṭīya*, p. 23

5 This sentence very closely resembles sura 114 of the Qur'an. See Mahfouz, *Ḥawla l-Dīn wa-l-Dīmūqrāṭīya*, p. 23

6 The Mother Book or Mother of the Book (*umm al-kitāb*) refers to the original source from which the Qur'an is derived. There is the belief within Islam that the Mother Book also has recorded within it all that has been and all that will be.

7 Mahfouz is here referring to Muhammad Iqbal (1877–1938), a poet and philosopher who is widely regarded as having inspired the Pakistan Movement.

> In Islam, prophethood attains its ultimate perfection in the recognition of the need for its own abolition. This contains the profound insight that existence cannot go on being dependent upon the rein that leads it forever; man, in order to achieve full knowledge of himself, must be left to rely upon his own devices.[8]

This means that man must not wait around for a new revelation, he must not depend upon a means of knowledge that resembles revelation in terms of its spontaneity and comprehensiveness; he must determine a function for his feelings and natural impulses unlike the functions of gnosis; from the intellect alone he must create the true, human path to knowledge. Religion will maintain its important existential role – its role of giving tutelage to the intellect, not suppressing it, restricting its sphere, or interfering in its endeavours – in the assurance of its utilisation for the good of man and existence, by acting as a deterrent against the temptations of ruin and perdition, and by its hoisting the banner of love under which intellectuals can find protection; they are wary of the conceited proclamations, the arrogance, the abuse, and the hopelessness. In this way the intellect will be made sacred, it will conquer the vastness of the world and establish its sublime truth, and life will be sanctified through rationality and worship simultaneously.

The other meaning of this is that it will bring out the noblest aspects of our humanity, exalting it. We will take an interest in science and the learned; we will confer upon them the station which God has chosen for them: they will be at the forefront occupying positions of leadership. We will provide them with what they deserve in terms of requirements, privileges, and means – and in pursuit of this we will spare no effort, sacrifice, or expense. This is what is required at the present time and what religion commands us to do.

This is natural within a religion that does not rely upon miracles alone but which is based upon contemplation, examination, and wisdom. This is natural within a religion which makes the pursuit of knowledge an obligation for all its believers, which exalts the station

8 Mahfouz does not provide a reference for this quotation.

of the learned, and which gives precedence to the knower over the worshipper.

Scientific Research

On the subject of research, I received a letter from Dr Mahmud Duwayr at the Max Plank Society in West Germany. He is an Egyptian researcher who was not encouraged by what he found in his scientific environment, so he emigrated to West Germany. I will set forth his valuable observations in what follows. I will not forgo this subject because I believe that it is the true foundation of the hoped-for awakening. Here are the observations of Dr Mahmud Duwayr:

1. It should not be overlooked that Egypt has a number of scientists who are capable of conducting scientific research in the most modern manner. However, Egypt, in its present state, is unable to provide them with the funds necessary for scientific research. The duty in this respect falls to the rich Arabs, either by supporting scientific research in Egypt or by establishing centres for research in their own countries for gifted, Arab scientists to work in.
2. Despite our economic difficulties in Egypt, it would be entirely feasible to achieve progress in scientific research if we focussed our efforts. This means focussing on a limited number of subjects which are demonstrably more advanced than others. If it is shown that the study of the fibres of wood and cotton is more advanced than the study of nylon and polyester, then it should be our first concern. In this case, the majority of the researchers would pool their expertise and talent, focussing on these specific subjects and be given what they require to conduct their research. As for the subjects, research will continue at its existing level or be furthered to the extent possible.
3. Researchers should not be given permanent positions at the scientific research institutes; rather, they should be given contracts which can be renewed – or not – in light of how

> effectively they perform. Subsequently, the researcher could be given a permanent position after his suitability has been confirmed.

These are the observations of Dr Mahmud Duwayr. It is our desire that he return to his country, along with the rest of our scientists who have emigrated, and establish temples for science in which no whisper of complaint is voiced and wherein the scientists, undisturbed, will devote themselves to clear thinking and diligent experimentation in the expanse of the love of truth.

A Tribunal!

In his letter to me, Professor Abdul Halim Husayn Abdul Halim at Mansoura University's Faculty of Medicine states:

> 'Poor and noble, and rich people are contemptible',[9] on the basis of this let us establish, of course, that by the former group we are referring to the Soviets, and by the latter, the Americans. It is clear from this, and from your writings in general, that a certain leaning has taken hold of your thinking. Sir, I would like to direct your attention to he who affirms the brutality of the human being, namely, Freud; and to he who affirms the brutality of history, that is, Karl Marx; as for the writer who calls for abuses to be committed, that is Jean-Paul Sartre. I suppose that you are not ignorant of the link that binds them together – it is that they are all Jews.

In response to your view, I would like to express the following remarks:

9 This appears to be a reference to a prior article by Mahfouz entitled 'Poor and Noble', which appears in this collection. The professor's response to Mahfouz seems to represent cynical paraphrasing of the original title.

1. If you have understood from my writings that I am a Marxist, then either I did not present my views well or you were hasty in judgement. I have repeatedly tried to be a Marxist but I could not – I abandoned this in the end. Nevertheless, in Marxism there are humanitarian principles and social justice that deserve admiration and respect. Furthermore, it has taught humanity many lessons that can be put to good use by anyone who so desires.
2. Let me make it clear for you that I do admire the Soviet Union, just as I also admire the United States; both have achieved stunning progress – achievements that are indispensible to humanity. This admiration, however, does not make me blind to their faults. Nevertheless, in comparing their negative aspects, I find that I have no other choice but to prefer the Soviet Union; whatever its faults may be, there is no racism in it, nor has it gotten involved in committing a crime against a nation in the magnitude of that committed by the United States in Vietnam. Furthermore, it did not perpetrate the greatest crime in the history of mankind: dropping the first two atomic bombs on human beings without there being a pressing need to do so, and thereby opening a door which may cause mankind's extinction as a result of annihilation.
3. Whatever your opinion about the school of psychoanalysis, Marxism, or existentialism, there is no doubt that Freud, Marx, and Sartre are among the most important intellectuals in the history of Western civilisation. One has the right to criticise their views and reject them, but that stage will not be reached unless we discuss them in an informed and objective manner. Regarding your portrayal of their philosophies as part of a global conspiracy hatched by the Jews in order to manipulate the world, all this does is show that you inflate the greatness of the Jews and their genius beyond what they merit, while diminishing the sagacity of the remainder of mankind, as though they are a plaything with which the Jewish genius amuses itself!

Furthermore, to the best of my knowledge Sartre is not a Jew, nor does he call for abuses to be committed; rather, he calls for engagement with humanity and its problems.

9 August 1976
AB

A Platform without a Distinguishing Characteristic

I have heard from more than one source that quite a few intend to nominate themselves as independents. These days the definition of an independent is someone who is not right wing, centrist, or leftist. Due to the remnants of the past, I was uncomfortable about the manner of independence, in terms of what it has formerly signified. This may be due to the role played by independents prior to the July Revolution. It seems that they considered themselves to be above joining with the old parties, distancing themselves from party conflict with grandiose abstemiousness, or abstemious grandiosity. The fact is, however, that they were simply incapable of courageously entering the fray, or of engaging with the public, or of daring to risk the defeats of battle. They sought refuge in what they termed independence while playing a cunning game amongst the parties, making deals with this one and that one, turning this one and that one to their advantage. Thus, they reserve themselves for civil coups so that they may become deputies and ministers.

What do you see as the benefit of independence today? What does it mean, and what is its objective? Let's try to clarify it. Perhaps it will lead us to the wisdom of its existence. So, what is the meaning of the independent?

1. Perhaps he is someone who did not find himself on the right, the centre, or the left. He belongs to a strange, passive independence that denies its adherent any identity and makes him

a person with no political characteristics, so that it is impossible for us to verify what he claims.

2. Perhaps he is someone who rejects the platforms and principles of the three, which the platforms are pledged to, and the socialist solution, and perhaps the Revolution itself, with its two known phases; he uses independence as a veil by which he conceals his rejection and his inner identity.
3. Perhaps he is someone who admires something of the right, something of the centre, and something of the left, and it was not possible for a platform to then fully hold him. So, he declares his independence in order to back the view that he admires, whatever its source, and he opposes that which does not appeal to him, whatever its source. In this case, he is pledged only to the three principles that the platforms are pledged to. These are the inevitability of the socialist solution, social peace, and national unity. This independence is positive as you can see, and it may perform a role when necessary; however, it can be invalidated with reflection and volition.

In all of these cases, nomination on the basis of being independent comes back to the election of the person on the grounds of his personal character, not as a representative of an opinion. In elections we want opinion to be prominent and the personality to be blotted out, so that the electoral contest will be purged of infatuation for the individual person, and so that its field accommodates the clash of opinions and principles.

Through a discussion with some of the personalities about this matter I have learned that they applied to join the organisation that they are in agreement with. However, it did not agree to their joining it, so they had no choice but to put themselves forward as a candidate in line with the principles of the organisation in the absence of its nominating them. This is a way of acting that bears the stamp of legitimacy and honesty, and which does not transgress the spirit desired for the new experiment.

We want to begin the new experiment with clarity regarding the ideas and attitudes so that we will be in harmony with an era which is sometimes called the era of principles, in which independency means only opportunism or loss of direction.

A Dialogue with Readers about Islam and the Battle of Ideologies

My remarks on Islam and the battle of ideologies excited the interest of many readers; I have accumulated an abundant number of letters from those who applaud my opinion and those who are critical in their rejection of it.

From the first group are the letters of Mr al-Husayni Ahmad Jalal (of El-Hamoul, Menofia), Mr Awad (a teacher in Tanta), Muhammad Abdullah (a dentist in Cairo), and Professor William Mikhail (a professor at the American University) – and in all of their letters there was a clear and enthusiastic call for:

1. The study of contemporary, political doctrines to be scientific and objective, without accusation levelling or revilements.
2. Studying the capacities of Islam to meet the age and its difficulties head on, and to create a modern, open society which provides advancement and prosperity for its people in an atmosphere of freedom, justice, and tolerance. If this column had the space for their letters, then I would publish them verbatim, for they deserve to be published, read, and absorbed.

As for the second group, these are letters from Messrs. Muhammad Sa'id Abul Kair (of Alexandria), Hamza al-Gami'i (the former director general at the Ministry of Finance), and Dr Muhammad Fathy al-Shadhili (of the Alexandria Faculty of Medicine).

A summarised version of Professor Muhammad Sa'id Abul Kair's letter:

1. A vehement attack on communism and the communist states, and the charge that its principles are utterly false.

2. An attack on communist agents in Egypt, how true Muslims resisted them when they – the agents – were in the centres of power, and how, because of this, the Muslims were subjected to punishment and torture.
3. Disdain towards drawing any parallels between Islam, as a divine religion, and democracy and communism, as two man-made doctrines – this being considered to be the first step on the road toward undermining the sublime Qur'an.

The professor has complete freedom to criticise communism, and so forth, as he sees it. However, he has a poor opinion of us, which is unwarranted – we called for discussion rather than revilement. Through study and comparison we desired that those in positions of authority acknowledge that, concerning the positive benefits for the good of man, Islam comprises what democracy and communism together comprise in terms of positive values, or that which surpasses them both. This will only come about through study, comparison, and persuasion, not by revilements and by antagonising the authorities. Among the learned works noted in this field is the book *Islamic Law as an Essential Source of the Constitution* by Dr Abdul Hamid Mutawali, and *Islam, Not Communism* by Dr Abdul Mun'im al-Namir – these two books are indispensible for anyone with an interest in this subject.

A summary of Professor Hamza al-Gami'i's letter:

1. The professor objected to a sentence which appeared in a previous article of mine, in which I spoke against the remarks of others and asked in astonishment: 'If Islam is as you say, then why did you not ask yourselves to come to it before calling us to do so?'[1] He commented upon this by saying: 'If this rejoinder is permissible for non-Muslims, it is not permissible for Muslims.' He viewed it as a criticism of Islam itself!

1 Unfortunately Mahfouz provides no reference to the article in which this quote appears.

2. He perfectly sums up the meaning of integrity in Islam: I do not see how the professor failed to see that my rejoinder was against Muslims – not Islam. He himself states in his message: 'I must first be clear that Islam is not a cause for the ignorance of Muslims and their decline. The true cause lies in the Muslims themselves, whose only affiliation to Islam is their birth certificate.' With these words the professor has provided my response for me.

A summary of the letter from Dr Muhammad Fathi al-Shadhili:

He cites sublime verses from the Noble Qur'an, among which, for the sake of example, is: 'And say, "The truth is from your Lord, so whoever wills – let him believe; and whoever wills – let him disbelieve."'[2] Then he presents his argument as follows:

1. Did these verses not provide clear proofs for a climate of tolerance for those who differ in opinion and belief?
2. The verses cited do not bring forth the outcry of the reviler and the incitement of the police as you say, good sir, in the article.

It is very clear – my good sir, and doctor – that the verses provide an atmosphere of tolerance for those who differ in opinion and belief, and it is also clear that they are far above the reviler and incitement of the police. But how was it that you thought that I charged Islam with bigotry or revilement in the message? My remark was directed towards Muslims, with regard to the fact that social intercourse is usually practiced in relation to Muslims – not Islam. In essence, what I am calling for is that the principles of Islam be effected through freedom, justice, tolerance, and so forth, so that a new society will be created in which there is no tyranny, no poverty, and no bigotry. In this way, the citizens, the people, and those who differ from us in opinion and belief, will live happily, not in word, but in deed. This was realised in a golden age: an age in which a frail Muslim made his defiance known to the caliph

2 Quotation from the Qur'an (18:29).

because he saw him strutting about in a new gown and he wanted to know what gave him the right to that; an age in which social security included Jews and Christians as beneficiaries, just as it did Muslims; an age in which Jews dared to attack the Qur'an, for it was content to debate with them and respond to them through the written word. What I want, sir, is action and conduct, not the quotation of sublime verses which we do not act in accordance with.

Concerning the New Communism

I received two letters concerning my remarks about the new communism in Europe:

The first is signed 'a reader'. In the new direction of the European communist parties he sees a deviation from the revolutionary script. He is astonished at my astonishment regarding the strong connection between justice within communist theory on one hand, and the materialist philosophy and the dictatorship of the working class on the other. He graciously provides an explanation of the theory as an integrated philosophy which I do not believe I can ignore – for this he deserves praise, at any rate. However, to the gentleman, I will not say that I was ever convinced regarding materialist philosophy or dictatorship as modes of governance, though I was convinced regarding justice. As long as you believe that justice is a self-evident truth you do not need a theory to support it, whereas the sempiternity of matter and the formation of consciousness during one of its stages are among those issues that require explanation and proofs which materialist theory does not provide. In any case, there are experiments before us being conducted in England and continental Europe, and any open-minded Marxist has a duty to follow them impartially and with a true, scientific spirit, so as to become aware of their results and to modify his position – should the matter require this – with the flexibility which characterises true, scientific thinking. Yet, I do regret the circumstances that forced the author of the letter to conceal his name, and I hope that life for him will extend to a future that will allow him to express his opinion in complete freedom and without impediment.

The second is signed 'Professor Hamid Yas', who is an academic. He says that the resolutions of the communist parties in Europe are only a kind of manoeuvre, nay a kind of plot rather, to pave the way for itself to rule, that it continues to harbour atheism and dictatorship, and that he fears that my defence of it will be considered a defence of Egyptian Marxists who invoke faith without any sincerity or genuine devotion.

The truth is that, without evidence, I cannot accuse a man of lying in a statement that he makes, just as I do not claim to know what lies in the hearts or that which is hidden. The advantage of this is that I presume the honesty of he who declares it, then I observe his actions with due vigilance. To believe the liar, in this case, is an error whose consequences can be rectified, but to accuse the truthful of lying is an inexcusable offence.

Austerity and Hygiene

Whenever we think about the austerity that the state has pledged itself to, the mind turns to visualising varieties of extravagance, such as subsidies for non-essential goods, or festivities and costumes, and so forth. However, hygiene is not visualised as one of these varieties, because hygiene is not a luxury; rather, it is, as has been said, at the heart of faith and the essential basis of health, beauty, and civilisation. Thus, it astonished me that Professor Mustafa Ghizlan (of Alexandria) would state in his letter that: 'Alexandria was cleaner before the imposition of the hygiene tax ... some of the cleaners are not receiving the minimum wage stipulated for all workers. Recently, in a session of the local council of the Governorate of Alexandria the subject of the required funds for the minimum wage was raised, particularly because they had already been incorporated into the plan of the estimated budget for the Governorate of Alexandria for 1976. However, the Ministry of Finance did not credit the stipulated amounts for the Governorate, which resulted in the deficit in the hygiene fund for Alexandria. Cleaning work must not be impaired, so that this is not reflected in public health, for we will be forced to bear a much greater cost combating epidemics and diseases than what we would have saved by the hygiene budget.'

If what is said in this letter is true, then it is a fair complaint, an accurate criticism, and an honest warning. Hygiene is a necessity in every town and village, let alone Alexandria, the port of the future and the summer resort for millions!

16 August 1976
AB

The Battle of Worries and Pacts

Our problems are innumerable. They include things about whose resolution there is no difference of opinion, such as the liberating of land and the establishment of a state for the Palestinians.[1] They include things about whose resolution there is agreement but which have been put off due to financial reasons, such as television and sewers. Then there are problems for which there can be a variety of views regarding the best solutions, such as the economic crisis or cleansing the country of corruption and the people involved in it. This last problem should be the crux of the election campaign, the number one issue for the electorate and the candidates, and then something that the new parliament will have to deal with out of respect for the will of the people.

Within the context of the economic crisis, some of us have learnt terms which have appeared for the first time such as economic liberalisation, the parallel market, and the free zones, and our hopes have also been pinned on aid, loans and support funds, etc. Some people object to this policy and reject it in whole or in part, or offer different ways of approaching the crisis. The election campaign is an opportunity for us to examine opposing views and to learn the best method for dealing with the crisis. Is this the only policy? Should some part of it be modified or completely changed? Can the crisis not be regulated without recourse to aid, loans, or funds, or by having recourse to one of these in the narrowest possible way? What should we do if aid and loans are

1 That is, the occupied Sinai Peninsula and Palestine.

withheld? Should we be living a lifestyle appropriate for a nation which is suffering the hardships we are going through?

Within the context of corruption, what should be done to put an end to the spectre gnawing away at our values and threatening productivity and progress? I mean that corruption which is born out of necessity during times of poverty and inflation, and the people who fall into it are those who find it hard to make ends meet. I do not bear those people any ill will, and may God forgive them, for that sort of behaviour is no more than a form of begging. I mean the large-scale corruption, the sort we read about with regard to the religious endowments administration,[2] the sort we read about with regard to the Cooperative Agricultural Union, and what we have read about regarding the commissions and other activities of the banks. The ramifications of that sort of corruption are not limited to individuals or a particular class, but extend to productivity and management; they upset the five-year development plan, and lay waste to people's efforts and hopes. This sort of large scale corruption sets a bad example for people who feel deprived, curious or even hesitant, and who then start practising it with the result that corruption spreads like water or air. We should like to see our parliamentary candidates promise to institute new and deterrent punishments commensurate with the magnitude of the evil which has come to the fore. Modern life needs new laws. Formerly, public funds were spent within a narrow remit, but today they are the foundation of development and anyone who drains them for his own use is not just weakening the present and the future of our country but also its very existence. Those people are worse for the country than saboteurs, murderers or arsonists, and based on this they must receive appropriate punishment. When it comes to the general security of the country, would you exploit its capabilities to the full?

---

2 Religious endowments administration (*awqāf*) refers to a system of religious endowments for the upkeep of buildings, schools or other charitable causes, which are theoretically unchangeable but which, due to inflation, are no longer viable due to the decrease in value of the original endowments.

Then there are the laws whose implementation no one seems to care about. Then there is the way the government treats its citizens which is an issue that does not need funding in order to be fixed but is a question of decisive and careful action.

The blame for a not-inconsiderable part of what we are suffering cannot be ascribed to a lack of hard currency, but first and foremost to negligence, thoughtlessness and indiscipline as well as the certainty that nothing is monitored, that there is no follow-up, and that no one is obliged to do his or her duty. So the election campaign should be an opportunity to uncover all the shortcomings in our lives which can be corrected through the force of will, and candidates should be made to agree to these reforms before being allowed to take up their positions in the new parliament.

Changing the World

An idea does not play its role in the history of humanity simply by dint of its being right, but it must change from being a thought that can be understood and is convincing to being a force that can influence affairs and relations, or, to put it in other words, that can have an effect on our general culture. In order for this risky change to come about, specific conditions must be created within society. An individual must arise who can breathe life into the idea and turn it into an influential and active force. Islamic civilisation discovered blood circulation, the philosophy of history and scientific procedures, but their effectiveness was only established hundreds of years later within the bosom of a different civilisation which developed them to the utmost degree.

Before the time of Christ there was a group of ascetic Jews who called for austerity, love and mercy, but they have left no trace among the Jews or in the world at large. When the messiah appeared everything changed. The torch was lit in people's hearts, their conscience was awakened, their concern for others was honed and innumerable early Christians were martyred. The old world started to crumble and in its place a proud new world arose.

More surprising than that was that this activity should have emerged with full force from an idea which not only was not subjected to sufficient scientific scrutiny but which might have turned out to be some fictional idea with no basis in intellectual veracity. However, influential and talented disciples were able to spread out with that magical and mysterious force of zealotry and obsession. The most recent example of that is National Socialism which was based on a completely anti-scientific form of racism but which found success due to certain social circumstances and the magic of a leader endowed with this mysterious force, which was, unluckily for mankind, also fallacious. By stating this I do not wish to diminish the importance of real ideas, God forbid, nor to underestimate the importance of imaginative thinking, but I do wish to state that just as mankind needs the light of truth, it also needs a force that can overcome obstacles and difficulties and create great works.

30 August 1976
RH

Wasted Potentials

It seems to me that it if we were to count the productive individuals – in the strict sense of the word 'productive' – then it would become evident to us that millions of our people are living off a minority of the population. In any given place you will come across wasted potentials that have no real impact on life, even though we are a developing country whose every inch needs a labouring hand or innovative thinking to alter its course and give it vitality so that it will bestow benefits and beauty. I say this: In any given place you will come across wasted potentials. You find that many of them are entirely out of work, begging, hunting around for their sustenance with resourcefulness and cunning, or performing petty services, such as cleaning car windows, or selling seeds, peanuts, and lottery tickets. You also find them in abundance – an abundance which is gradually rising – in government agencies and institutions, in their disguised idleness which delivers no result or service. If this were to be as an outcome of our needs having been fulfilled in terms of activity and work, then it would be of little importance and be seen as inevitable. But this is not the case. It is taking place as we complain of severe shortages in the various trades and professions, in commerce, metalworking, construction, and in the electrical and health professions. We complain about a great shortage in the number of professional teachers and skilled workers, and those who would utilise them to eradicate illiteracy in a planned and systematic way. No one is ignorant of these facts, nor do I believe that they are concealed from the sight of the officials. Despite this, however, we have continued to fall short in addressing them and finding a proper solution for them; indeed, we are actively making them worse with new, additional forms of bad practice. As an example, it was a matter of necessity that the technical institutes and training centres be able to accommodate 75 percent of the young people for schooling – only those possessing outstanding abilities with regard to the scientific disciplines were to be steered towards university. Likewise, there was also the need to forbid begging, or menial jobs, to all but the old and the disabled, and that the others be recruited at centres for training which would enable them to gain useful work at home or abroad. We should have fulfilled our need for teachers – for the schools and the eradication of illiteracy – utilising the qualified government employees, of which there are too many. We talked and talked and talked, but did nothing until the countryside began complaining about the lack of labour! Indeed, at times the need for agricultural labour becomes severe, yet it cannot be found. This is not because of an exodus; rather, it is because the young men of the village scorn agricultural labour once they begin attending school. They should have been studying during the winter and working in the summer, so that no damage would have been incurred – in this there would have been merit and honour. At the same time we find dozens of young men from the villages working as office boys, couriers, and hospital orderlies in rural government agencies, preferring salaried idleness to productive agricultural work. In this they seek the help of those in authority; indeed, at times the state has provided this for them when it decided to carry out the wishes of some of those discharged from the army. They choose petty governmental posts, shunning their original work of cultivating the land. Despite what is said about our resources with regard to agricultural land, minerals, energy sources, tourism, and the Suez Canal, it is our human potential that will remain at the forefront of these resources. There can be no objection to exporting the surplus of this potential on the condition that this benefits the country in some way, and provided that it will be replenished by others through a comprehensive plan of training and enablement.

In the absence of organisation and planning, the present situation is causing the exodus of thousands and thousands of workers, professionals, and technicians, to countries abroad, and the rampant shortages within the trades and professions, while huge numbers are wasted through disguised idleness and beggary at home. This is something unimaginable, especially during a time of planning and crises. Lately, we have begun to read in the newspapers about the activities at the Ministry of Manpower with regard to the establishment of vocational training centres and about their lack of equipment. We have also read about the modernisation of the teaching and education system – news that is cause for hope, even if it is late in coming. Truly, my hope is that the officials in these spheres work with the total conviction that they are investing in – what is, without question – our most important resources, and that they provide a solution for our economic crisis whose effectiveness will exceed all of the support funds.

Religious Aberration

Recently the security forces uncovered an aberrant religious group whose misguidance is carried out by cunning individuals who have selfish aims. I do not believe that we have forgotten the military academy affair yet, with its aberrants and its victims.[1] Aberration in the religious sphere, therefore, verges on constituting a social phenomenon. Religious aberration mainly arises from the exploitation of a class among the youth, or a great many of them, that tend towards the religious spirit. They turn people who aspire to goodness, piety, and love, into infatuated killers. With regard to strengthening the religious inclination among the youth, this is an inclination towards liberation and values in a world that is driven by corruption and opportunism. But why do the young people not find that which will satisfy their

1 This seems to refer to the 1974 attack on the Military Technical Academy in Cairo. The attack was carried out by members of the Islamic Liberation Organisation under the leadership of Salih Sirriya. Their hope had been to seize weapons and assassinate President Anwar Sadat who was attending an official event nearby, thereby triggering an Islamic revolution. The group was intercepted by security forces before they could leave the academy, however, with the ensuing battle leaving 11 dead and 27 wounded.

noble desires in the religious instruction that they receive in the various stages of education? Why do they not find this in radio broadcasting, television, and the newspapers, when these are not devoid of religious programmes? Why does Al-Azhar not provide them with it through its imams who are prevalent in the mosques, and by the other means at its disposal?[2]

It is clear that the aberrants did not find what would satisfy them and guide them on the right path in these quarters. It is easy for the tendentious to possess them, lead them astray, and to erect the spirit of evil and sin within them. There is also a likelihood that these quarters are not conveying their message as they should; perhaps something is lacking, perhaps they are concerned with some things at the expense of neglecting others, perhaps they have not yet arrived at the correct approach, or the appropriate language, to address all of the youth.

It is inconceivable, in my opinion, that it will suffice to identify the aberrants and those gone astray, and then present them before the courts; rather, there must be a dialogue between them and the men of Al-Azhar, and others among the men of education who are responsible for the religious lessons, not only for the purpose of guiding them, but also for the benefit of finding out the reasons for the aberration, and for a review concerning the manner of religious study, of the religious sermon, and the religious programmes. A dialogue may reveal other destructive factors outside the sphere of religion and the distinguished men thereof, factors that have been incubated by the general economic crisis, the rampant opportunism among the powerful, and the absence of a good example that is appropriate for the time and place, all of which curdles the blood of the innocents among the young people and inclines them toward extreme reactions and the directives of the clever deceivers. This dialogue might also reveal the particular concerns of the youth, such as sex, housing, the future, marriage, salaries, education, and culture, as well as their general concerns, such as aberration, hypocrisy, and corruption. And how is it that they did not hear a voice

2 Al-Azhar was founded in Cairo in the 10th century. It is one of the oldest and most prestigious centres of religious learning in the Middle East.

of religion, whether with regard to their particular concerns or general ones? It is as though the voice of religion was occupied with blind moralising, reminiscences of the past, political battles, and the struggle to implement the punishments of Islamic law.

It is my opinion that the dialogue which I am proposing would undoubtedly achieve something good for all parties concerned.

20 September 1976

AB

Times of Salvation

It is part of our inherent character to be over-excitable. When we are stirred by something important, we feel as if there is a burning brand in our heart and we become so immediately worked up that an onlooker may feel that we are about to change the world or recreate it. An outburst like this can last days or weeks and then as suddenly as it flared up it dies down and the reason for it becomes mired in oblivion. If the cause of this outburst is rape, or rape accompanied by murder, you will find sensational headlines in the newspapers and the talk in the coffee shops will be of nothing else. Threats will pour forth from the mouths of officials, and men of religion and lay people will come up with all sorts of contradictory suggestions, with the whole spectacle lasting for days. Then absolutely nothing will happen or a committee will be formed to look into the matter after which the whole thing will melt away into the deepest oblivion. The same thing will happen if a violent robbery takes place on a bus, if someone is evicted from their home in a brutal manner, or if the owner of a building assaults someone looking for an apartment, and so on and so forth.

Excitability is not the only defect in our general behaviour. There is another defect which spreads its poison, so to speak, into our life through our kith and kin, and that is indolence, sluggishness, indifference, or the lack of a sense of duty. These days this has been given a new name which is bone idleness. It is a defect which a sly person uses to screen his own shortcomings by claiming that it is caused by the absence of the appropriate law, the scarcity of hard currency, bureaucracy, or a lack of manpower, with no end of grumbling or complaining. The truth is that the first and essential deficiency is firmly implanted within such a person. He refrains from making any effort, and when there is no one there to check on him or impose any form of punishment he works at less than full capacity. I shall endeavour to present a real or an almost real picture of what you can find in any of the various spheres of activity. Anywhere there is an existing mode of behaviour of work, a sly person will see it the way he wants to. It has become run of the mill for us to accept the status quo as unchangeable, for us to demand things to be the way they should be, but have we truly asked ourselves whether we have actually benefited from all the possibilities of the status quo? Have we decided not to pass any new legislation, change our relationships or regulations until we have ascertained that the old has completely served its purpose and proved its inability to cope with modern times?

In this respect we need to follow a softly-softly policy with prudence and wisdom. We have to make the government machinery swing into action when necessary, and if there is still a loophole after that, we need to reformulate the regulations in order to plug it. When it comes to crime and criminality how many unused laws do we have! We might even say that we suffer from a surfeit rather than a lack of laws, and it feels as if those charged with putting them into action and protecting the population are permanently out for lunch. In days gone by you could always find a soldier or a watchman in the street. The cities, and particularly Cairo, have become overcrowded and there is a lack, so to speak, in the number of soldiers; for longer than I can remember I have not seen a patrol or a policeman in whole neighbourhoods, but can we really not use the power and laws we have before setting off to promulgate new laws which I fear will meet the same fate as those we already have?

We are not short of laws, nor armed authorities, nor manpower, and these are all subject to the higher authority of the courts, administrative censorship, the Court of Audit and the anti-corruption authority. What we lack in the short term – and let us not think here about the education and perseverance we need for the long term – can be summed up in the word 'resoluteness'. We need a resoluteness that does not differentiate between a minister and a watchman and which comes down harshly upon those who behave fecklessly, in order to assuage the honest citizens, in the gentle penumbra of a free press and a parliament which we hope will act for welfare and progress.

27 September 1976

RH

A Battle and Men

The three organisations have nominated their men, and the others have put themselves forward as independents. The battle now turns on the election of the Assembly, which we hope will be the pillar of democracy in Egypt. We have known from the start that it will not be an absolute democracy as long as it operates within the framework of the three principles: the inevitability of the socialist solution, social peace, and national unity. However, we also know that these three principles do not constitute a restriction on democracy which would corrupt its essence or transgress its function. A system of control will not realise social peace and national unity like a democratic system would, with its ample freedoms, its opening up of the way for every voice to be heard and for every right of every individual or group to be safeguarded. With regard to the inevitability of the socialist solution, it is a restriction outwardly only; it does not restrict the people, but restricts he who would be tempted to exploit the people. Here socialism defends democracy against the economic freedom that deprives the masses of social justice and purges any real substance from the freedoms afforded by it. For those who have read the placards and posters it will be obvious that the focus remains on the personal characteristics of the candidate, not the principles. Maybe this is due to the overlapping of principles and their convergence, or because the placards and posters do not have the space to explain the principles and programmes. Perhaps it would be useful if each organisation were to sketch its own particular characteristics – those which distinguish it from the other two organisations – and promulgate them continuously, or semi-continuously, until the day of the election. If we were to take up the proposal to elect from candidate lists with proportional representation, then we could broaden the range of principles at the expense of personalities and provide the opportunity for a new political education, especially in the countryside.

Now let's take a look at the battle map. The first thing that confronts us is the organisation of the centre. Its strength is evident in its solidity, coordination, and its vigour. As for its being official, or semi-official, this will not influence the will of the voter according to past evidence, both recent and further back. Perhaps the underlying cause of its real power is in its representing the principles of the July Revolution (23 July and 15 May), and in its moderateness, which is in accord with the nature of our people, generally speaking. There is no doubt that its winning a majority will ensure stability and development, which would be for the better.

After this comes the organisation of the right. This represents a reaction towards the negative aspects of the past, but it confuses the negative aspects of the system for the system itself. Thus, it calls for the private sector to be unleashed from all restrictions; indeed, it calls for a system whose good points and bad points have been put to the test – and the experience demonstrated that its bad points outweigh its good ones. We are not against the private sector provided that it pursues the development plan with the leadership of a revived public sector which is freed from negative aspects. In any case, it is our hope that the organisation will achieve a success commensurate to its size amongst the people, so that it represents a strong opposition – something without which democracy cannot exist.

Then there is the organisation of the left. It is noticeable that it has only made nominations for a limited number of districts, and this does not correspond with its intellectual importance. This may have been due to the impact of the campaign which accused the organisation of atheism, despite the fact that there are notable people within it who represent the religious, Islamic mainstream. It is our hope that the organisation succeeds in becoming a base of opposition so that the new Assembly represents the political currents.

Lastly, there are the independents. In putting themselves forward, they usually rely on their personal characteristics and their national record. I previously stated an opinion about the meaning of independence, and I have received letters – from Messrs. Muhammad Fahmi Tawfiq (a lawyer), Abdul Fattah al-Sayr Inani (a Bachelor of Journalism), Yahya Muhammad al-Batl (a pharmacist), and Kamil Mansur Muhammad (from the customs house in Alexandria) – which discuss my opinion frankly and openly. It can be said that they prefer independence due to their lack of confidence concerning the experience of the platforms put forward. Of course, they are entitled to take the position which agrees with them; however, by presenting their national record or putting forth their programmes they will reveal particular credentials that would link them to the centre, the right, or the left. Perhaps this would justify, in the event of their success, their joining one of the three organisations, if they find this to be a fulfilment of the public interest and not a hostile act against the will of the voters who elected them after their credentials had become known, and despite their independence from the organisations when nominated.

Whatever the outcome the elections produce, we will have a People's Assembly, by which I hope that we will write the life history of a stable, successful democracy.

The Bitter Reality

A letter from Muna, a young lady from Alexandria, overflows with bitterness, indignation, and anger. It almost bursts into flames between one's fingers from the intensity of its emotion, the fire of its passion, and the horror of its vision. She is a graduate from one of the occupational colleges. She shares a chair with a female colleague of hers in the same department because of severe overcrowding; nevertheless, she spends the entire working day without work. With sorrow she recalls dreams of studying, the golden hopes of serving the nation, the beautiful slogans that she memorised by heart. She recalls this as she plunges into a rough, harsh reality wherein there is no grace, no beauty, and nothing good; the streets are filled with rubbish and sewage, and the prospect of the queues keep her awake at night: queues of tormentors outside institutions and stations of transportation. She curses falsehood, hypocrisy, cowardice, and the destruction of security. She does not know how to escape from these, since they assail her in every place; just as news of robberies and torture in the newspapers assail her; just as fools assail her in the streets asking: 'What have I gained from a civilisation seven thousand years old?'

Thus, the birds will inevitably migrate. These are excerpts of her words. They depict the terrible fall of youth from the top of its ivory tower to the bottom of reality, with its sharp teeth. Let us ask the unavoidable question: What can a young person do when faced with this reality? The anticipated response consists of three possibilities:

1. He can adapt himself to it and accept his disgraceful nationality.
2. He can flee from it to a better place.
3. He can try to change it as much as he can while sticking to his principles.

Obviously, the first possibility is inadmissible. As a general rule, the second cannot be commended; it may be a solution for an individual, or individuals, but it will be a temporary one, and it will not change the status quo. Whatever incidental benefits it may achieve, it is a heavy national loss, especially since it is normally only the select – those qualified in science and craft – who can go abroad.

Nothing remains except the last possibility, which is the attempt to change the situation while upholding principles. It is the noble mission of this generation – and perhaps it is the noble mission of every generation – and any thought of turning away from it means turning away from obligation, duty, and from life's meaning, value, and purpose. Criticism alone is not sufficient, and complaining alone is weakness and impotence. There must be labour, and the labour might be great, such as commitment to the principles of a party, or it might be small, such as calling medical assistance for someone who has fallen unconscious, but labour all the same – it will be no use without it.

Duty compels me to direct two remarks:

The first is directed to the important men in education and the media. It is naive of us to portray the world and people to children in an ideal, rosy manner, like rose water; they should know many facts of human nature and social relations according to the reality, without falsification and embellishment, so that they collide with truth at the first encounter. Indeed, in this regard I recall the attacks that I have faced in my literary life because of the realism of my novels. How often I have been accused of disagreeable forwardness! How often I have been accused of pessimism! How often I have been urged to beautify reality! Here we have a pure young woman, but she is also a victim of exaggeration and falsehood.

The second is to Muna, the author of the letter: Miss, I hope that you abandon some of your idealism – and not a small part of it. The society which you look down upon is one that has suffered much from iniquity, war, poverty, and crises. Do not expect it to be a pretty picture of cleanliness, elegance, and good health. Know that the best of people – along with the rest – are made up of fierce impulses and that they contain a dreadful measure of selfishness, vanity, and greed. And know that their evil sides grow more wicked in bad conditions, when the economy worsens and there is a shortage in all services.

You must be fair in your judgement of people; they deserve kindness as much as they deserve criticism and anger. I am not saying this so that you tolerate wickedness or ally yourself to it, not at all, but so as to stir the reservoirs of love in your heart which anger has filled. Through love one's outlook undergoes a change; you would refrain, perhaps, from emigrating, you would think seriously of doing something. The weight and scale of whatever that may be is not what is important, what matters is that it is a rain, even if only a droplet of aid for the sake of the desired change. Moreover, know that the change is coming – there is no doubt about it – and that the efforts expended for its sake are not insignificant. Finally, let me ask you a question: What was the state of the Russian people following the German invasion? And what was the state of the German people following the invasion of the Russians, the English, and the Americans? And what is the state of these two peoples today?

18 October 1976

AB

Doctrine and Example

I was sitting early one morning in the Café de La Paix, in half solitude by the sea. The fresh air should have cleared my head and relaxed me had it not been that the newspaper reports of the various investigations into torture and corruption had the completely opposite effect on me. That was how I was feeling when a respectable-looking old man sat down in front of me; smiling as if in apology, he introduced himself. He turned out to be a venerable professor at the Alexandria Faculty of Medicine. Before I could say a word, he launched into conversation with me:

'What do you think? Which is more important for a doctor, science or ethics?'

I was astonished at the way he just blurted out the question and thought that he must have been mulling the subject over for a long time. Perhaps he had been having an incessant dialogue with himself on a subject which was troubling him and was voicing his inner conversation. He did not wait for my answer. He did not give me a chance to think it over but stated:

'Ethics are everything.'

Courting controversy, I wondered aloud: 'What is the purpose of ethics without the requisite knowledge or skill?'

He answered authoritatively: 'Ethics oblige a man to acquire knowledge and to keep on doing so until the end of his life. An ethical man is simultaneously an educated man, or should be.'

I declared my sincere amazement at the thought, and he continued recounting anecdotes of professional misdemeanours and then muttered ruefully: 'What times we live in!'

In an attempt to console him, I replied: 'The phenomenon is as rampant as a plague. The important thing is for us to treat it.'

'That's true. We have to start from the family and school.'

'And how can we guarantee the well-being of the family and school? Aren't family and school just two units of the society we are speaking about? Most importantly we should know the reasons.'

'And what are the reasons according to your way of thinking?' he asked deep in thought.

'One of them is unarguably the financial crises, by which I mean the spectre of inflation. In inflationary times the principle of necessity prevails, not that of a higher purpose.'

'And another is the shocking behaviour of some civil servants for there can be no integrity in the wider society without them setting a good example and nor can there be real accountability if they lack integrity.'

Then, with a frown, he said: 'You are just exacerbating the difficulties.'

'And what's more, behind all that there is something more important and dangerous, for ethics do not grow out of a vacuum. The source of ethics is beliefs and schools of thought whether they are religious, political or philosophical. Before the Corrective Revolution the state expended huge efforts to eradicate certain beliefs and schools of thought, and to persecute ideologues of all varieties until only the unaffiliated and the opportunists remained, and their particular ethics which stem from self-serving egotism. That is how the prisons filled up with beliefs, and the fabric of society was plunged into decadence.'

We exchanged a sad smile with each other and I continued: 'We want an ideology. We want an example.'

The respectable old gentleman asked: 'How do we begin?'

'We have actually already started,' I said calmly. 'We started when we gave the press its freedom, the law its supremacy and the people their pulpits, for what follows night but dawn.'

A Successful Film

The engineer, Ali Iffat, wrote me a letter asking what it is that makes a film a success, what role the actors play in this, and what role publicity plays. I can reel off many reasons for a film's success, but whatever the reasons may be for the factors behind a film's success, no single one can be termed a recipe for success – although you might identify one of these elements in a film destined to be a flop. I will, therefore, avoid subjectivity on this matter and say that a good film is one which causes the public to respond to the theme as a whole, that is, to like it because it strikes a chord in their thoughts and subconscious. The public does not respond to the subject matter separately from other filmic elements such as the direction, the acting, the cinematography, the editing, the film sets and the dialogue. These have only a subliminal effect on all but the small number of film aficionados. The overwhelming majority of filmgoers take the theme to be an extension of their lives. They experience the film and discuss it as if it were real, not fiction. There then arises the issue of how the public can be guided towards the best film? How can they discern this among the scores of films on general release? Here the role of the supporting factors comes in. I say supporting inasmuch as a film's real success is established by the theme, but these supporting factors are also based on an appeal to the grassroots in the full meaning of the term, and this grassroots appeal, which helps steer the public to their favourite subject matter, must be backed up with film star appearances, publicity, and the right choice of distributor and screenings, etc.

It goes without saying that the film stars are the single most important element; their appearance in a film gives it a peerless power of attraction and has a captivated public rushing to see it in the certain knowledge that they will not be disappointed. Film stars, however, cannot turn a bad film into a successful one. The proof of that is that we applaud a star in a good film, just as we applaud him in a bad one, but his role is crucial in attracting an audience. If the theme is critically acclaimed, the star gets the credit, but if it is a flop the film does not detract from his talent and people think he just made a bad choice in appearing in it. Thus, a good film is one with a good theme, but a good theme can get lost in the multitude of films on release unless it has a star who is a prime attraction. We often hear people speak of the need to free films from being star vehicles, but what other way is there of attracting a large audience to a film when the only thing that matters to them is the matinee idol star? A director has a handful of fans, the writer scores or hundreds, but the star, male or female, is the true hero of the cinema and the theatre.

22 October 1976
RH

Important Matters

We know that the government will present its detailed proposals to the People's Assembly after the Eid al-Adha holiday. Special committees will study them and then they will be presented for discussion by the nation's parliamentarians. It will be an opportunity for the new People's Assembly to scrutinise matters which both concern and pain the homeland, and to come up with solutions which will work in both the short and long term. As these pressing concerns are numerous I should like to cast a glance at some concerns of no less, and perhaps even greater, seriousness, although they generally take a back burner compared to the suffering of the masses, and public services, etc.

The Aswan High Dam

Everything possible, positive and negative, has already been said about this and I have stopped following the debate or reading the various statements issued by the National Council for Productivity out of a strong conviction of the dam's importance and greatness and because all the pros and cons have long been stated. Had it not been for the consequences of the consecutive wars, all our projects would have been completed on time, but our inability to do so has exposed the shores, dams and the waters of our Nile to an unimaginable setback. In order to avoid further delays, we need to see a precise and scientific inventory so that we can know what has actually been done to get the projects back online, what has not yet been carried out and when we will start rectifying matters. The picture has to be clarified in all its dimensions and we need to know what is still to be done, for the future and security of the dam is the security and future of Egypt.

Academic Research in Egypt

I do not need to say that without real support for the scientific establishment, no reform or progress will provide the groundwork for originality, credibility or success. For that reason we should not be grudging with funding, however much it takes. I am well aware that the greatest possible efforts are being expended but these efforts fall far short of the mark. We need resources and equipment, incentives and good conditions for researchers. We need to create the appropriate environment and conditions for university professors to be able to prioritise their scientific writing rather than seeing them posted here and there and having to invigilate at examinations. We need to listen to dedicated teachers such as Dr Shukri Ibrahim Sa'ad, a professor of biology at the Faculty of Science in Alexandria, who sent me a warm and credible letter about his scientific research and teaching in which he expressed the most sincere hopes of those who wish to see their homeland become a beacon for humanity, hopes which will only become a reality through dedicated application and innovation in science.

Education

This is a strange case. There is not a single person who is not aware of the shortcomings and mistakes of teaching today, and who does not lampoon its backwardness. However, teaching goes on as normal and produces its consequences year after year while we discuss the matter and make suggestions but get no closer to eradicating the roots of the disease. Education has become more accessible for the children of the masses thanks to the Revolution, and it is also free, but we know that it is not education as education should be, and it is not free except for those who cannot afford the special fees and they generally drop out at some stage of their education. Primary education does not include all children, and many fail to complete it. With regard to those who have the opportunity to continue their education, they suffer from educational practices which do not encourage free thinking or innovation or socialise children effectively. The students then take part in a wild scramble for a place at colleges, most of which, due to overcrowding, have become no more than high schools and are about as far from a university as they can be in spirit and in terms of aims. Then, the moment they graduate, their whole educational training becomes as nought as they find jobs in the civil service or the private sector which has no need for them and no work for them either.

That is the reality at a time when the desired aim of education is to get the street sweepers back to doing academic research and for every individual to do work for which he is qualified.

Labour

Labour, or human resources, is our greatest treasure and is closely connected to the question of education, but it suffers from special problems which affect absolutely everyone. In order to arrive at a decent solution there are some general principles which we absolutely and unavoidably must accept:

1. No government or public sector place of employment should have a single superfluous employee or worker.
2. No government or public sector place of employment should lack an employee or worker.
3. Any glut of employees should be used to bolster the number of anti-illiteracy teachers, be sent to work aboard, or be trained in professions which complain of a lack of workers at all levels.

These are vital issues whose fate should not be overlooked amid the plethora of other pressing concerns.

Censorship and Film Certification

Mahmud al-Darini, from the Faculty of Law, Alexandria, asked me about film censorship and why it does not express a more influential opinion on the level of a film, why flops are allowed to be shown, as well as other artistic questions regarding films which receive authorisation to be screened.

Censorship is essentially interested in limited moral, religious and political values, which are subjective, and in the easily noticeable aspects on which a position can be taken. Generally the ministers involved scrutinise the artistic values and try to submit them to censorship also by bending the old censorship law to their aims. In discussion they throw up significant obstacles, including the claim that artistic values by their very nature have aroused such sharp differences of opinion that it is almost impossible to agree about a film's artistic merit. This leads to innumerable examples of differences of outlook and taste, even at a global level. Not even William Shakespeare or Ahmed Shawqi are free from that if we accept that, in principle, we face a new obstacle especially with regard to the people appointed to judge the merit of works who issue their favourable or negative judgements regarding the authors and literary works of Egypt.

It is true that there are some people who work in the field of censorship who are in fact qualified and have some degree of expertise, but when a great writer faces negative opinions from his compatriots this causes some grief, as is obvious to the astute. In order to avoid this some ministers have formed a supreme council of censorship made up of well-known intellectuals, but this committee has been operating for years under a ministerial decree and not in accordance with the law. It has obviously faced some hardships which have stymied the purpose of its existence, proof of that being that awful films have not disappeared and actually constitute most of the cinematic output. In addition to that, we are entering a new era of freedom with which the shackles of censorship are not in accord. On the one hand, we should allow the public to be the judges and critics, and on the other hand we should encourage new films in a plethora of ways. Thereafter, we should remember that art is one of the manifestations of civilisation and that in the final analysis the level of a country's artistic output is related to the ups and downs of civilisation, and that it is unreasonable for us to make demands of art alone which we do not make of the rest of cultural activities. I do not say this in order to confirm my concerns but as a call for justice and fairness. There are other calls which I direct to the critics and government officials to make them apply their most constructive criticism and encouragement for the rebirth of art at an appropriate level.

Literati and the Youth

In a letter from Mr Osama Anwar Okasha there are some wise and inclusive words regarding the crises of literature, analysing at the same time his own personal crisis as he analyses scores, or, if you like, hundreds, of other crises affecting the young literary public in Egypt. His, however, remains an individual case with ever increasing elements of strangeness. He started his journey at the beginning of the sixties, and over the course of three consecutive years he won six literary awards, published excellent short stories in the press, and even had a collection of stories published by the Supreme Council for the Promotion of the Arts and Literature in the summer of 1967. In 1973 he was awarded a grant and he wrote a novel which now occupies its place among the scores of short stories in the drawers of his office and which has remained unknown, with him unable to find a publisher or readers.

His is a much sinned-against talent which has proved its power and energy and despite all the encouragement from the Supreme Committee and the Ministry of Culture, it has been unable to grow, develop or take its rightful place. I know many similar talents which are still locked away in drawers with only a small minority of them finding their way into the public domain after much effort by the artists and people trying to promote them, and with no financial gain whatsoever, or occasionally because an Iraqi publisher has expressed his appreciation. Only rarely, however, do these published works appear in the Egyptian book market.

It must be said that the reading public bears some part of the responsibility for this situation, but some blame for the public's literary lethargy can be ascribed to a more inclusive phenomenon which is the stagnation of the literary movement in recent years. We do not even discuss this phenomenon any more, believing it to be temporary, although it is on its way to becoming permanent. However, we must discuss the policies of the state cultural sector. We must start by recognising that there are quite a few annual literary prizes and we have no comment to make about this, but to date the state cultural sector has not instituted a solid policy for dealing with new or young talent. It has complete control of magazine and book publishing, the theatre, cinema, radio and television – which are all forms of media which young talent can only reach after enormous effort and after overcoming almost impenetrable obstacles in most cases or perhaps with recourse to methods which are devious at best. The only solution for this problem is to put in place a robust policy aimed at uncovering new talent, to publicise this talent within the right artistic arena, and to insist on it being promoted provided it has proven artistic merit so that this new talent can find its appropriate artistic level.

22 October 1976

RH

A Murderer and a Murderess

In two consecutive instances a murderer and a murderess have been arrested on similar charges, but different in terms of causes and manner. With regard to the murderer, the causes for his crime had been set for him since his birth: he grew up in poverty, and his father treated him harshly and threw him out. He ended up in a reformatory which extinguished his humanity and goodness; it filled him with hatred, a sense of alienation, and a lust for revenge. He came to embody the various defects of his family and society. The reformatory moulded him into a harmful pest; it committed aggression against innocence without hesitation and shed the blood of its victim with demonic coldness. He stood gaunt and unconcerned, regarding his deed with coldness and indifference. The public were outraged by the crime, not only because of its savagery, but also because many saw in it the embodiment of their neglect and passivity, and the ugliness and mutilation nourished by their society. There was an impetuous desire to execute the criminal as quickly as possible, so that he disappear from their life, as a witness of them and their worn out, rotten life. No one thought of taking the father into account, nor hastened to consider personal status law, and no one thought of investigating those in charge at the reformatory, because the important thing was that, first and foremost, the witness disappear and that the feelings of guilt subside.

As for the murderess, other motives were in play: soft motives, like ambition for wealth and status, and the service of those with status and expensive tastes. She is a killer, in a figurative sense. She did not murder a child or a youth, she murdered values and ruined reputations.

She did not commit her crimes in an old abandoned house, but in luxury apartments and elegant villas. Her deed aroused curiosity and smiles; the people saw in her a representation of their own aspiration, inclination, and craving in this world. Moreover, they found in her a faithful servant that had fallen and who performed her duty in raising their spirits.

The murderer is a bitter fruit of an ailing society teeming with children and the unfortunate. They face life in extreme living conditions, expending continual effort to procure food, clothing, and civilisation. They face hardship in obtaining the minimum of those things needed for life and provide the nation its finest sons: students, soldiers, and workers. But some of these individuals may face very bad conditions; they become aberrant and commit brutal crimes that are marked by bitterness, suffering, and despair.

The murderess is the fruit of another society, but the overwhelming majority of this society are bitter fruits. They are a gang that possesses great power, influence, and authority, and which commits its crimes both secretly and openly. The people joke about their extraordinary ventures in the markets of smuggling, embezzlement, bribery, pimping, prostitution, and corruption. They talk of their fantastical riches, their daring raids, and their unrivalled brazenness. They profit without consideration and they spend without consideration, and they trample values and laws without consideration. If one of them falls due to a stumble of fortune, or a careless slumber, he lands on his feet – indeed, haughtily – as the pundits rush to his defence, and care and concern surround him. So you see, we are two nations, not one: a nation living in opulence, immersed in luxury, and a developing nation toiling as part of the third world.

17 November 1976

AB

The Philosophy of the State Radio and Television

The policy of opening up the domain of intellectual debate has had a lasting influence on people. I have not come across anyone who has not spoken to me about the party or press conferences. For the first time state television has been broadcasting opposing views and daring thoughts regarding state policy, encouraging listeners and viewers to think for themselves, to draw comparisons, hold discussions and derive real enjoyment from the blessing of freedom. For the first time interest in political debate is matching the magical power of radio and television. This is a power which is never far from my mind but it is only rarely that I have found it as vividly embodied as I do now. The broadcast media are the most powerful means of expression, more powerful than a book, newspaper or cinema. They are played permanently in every house, cafe or club and in many other places via the transistor radio. But have we given enough thought to using this power for the good of mankind and society? Sometimes it seems to me like the 'thousand varieties' you can find in the shops. It is a useful and enjoyable form of progress and often you think it is useful and enjoyable as it represents a carefully selected form of taste, one that the listeners demand or what the state officials have indicated, but it is one in which no clear strategy or defined philosophy has crystallised. It may be for this reason that the media are not devoid of contradictions or incongruities and, hence, we may see a religious programme followed almost immediately by one showing a scantily-clad dancer, or an intellectual discussion followed by a programme with a palm reader or astrologer.

I ask myself the following question: Can we not dedicate chosen principles or a specific philosophy for our broadcast media? Principles which take into consideration the culture and entertainment presented from children's programmes to those for older viewers and adults. Let us set aside politics, external and internal, for that has its own special conditions and specific influencing factors. I am more interested in what affects the individual, what forms or reforms him, in the domain of which we are speaking – the media – regardless of other factors which may be even more influential such as the economy and education, etc. The desired form of an individual is that which includes the living heritage in his make-up along with an endeavour to equip the viewers fully for modern life. That is what should drive the conscience of every media personality, what should be done instinctively, and what every executive should believe in and work to achieve whether he is making a serious or entertainment programme, when he debates and discusses, when he is playing and joking, when he speaks words of wisdom, proverbs and stories, or when he tells jokes or anecdotes. It should not be difficult for us to call for the good in our heritage and in modern times to be brought together, but we have to face the problem of choosing. What should we take from tradition and what should we set aside? Which aspects of modern culture should we follow and which should we avoid? The matter needs serious thought, discussion and contemplation, but there are general principles which I hope will not be the subject of argument, such as:

1. Religious values – by religion, I do not mean just rituals, precepts and laws, I mean the eternal humanistic message which sanctifies the individual, has room for deliberation, aims for social justice and calls for brotherhood, love, peace and tolerance among human beings irrespective or their religion, colour or race, and which despises hatred, extremism or decadent attitudes.
2. Selected traditional values, which are the produce of the intellect and conscience, which have validity for all times and places, and which respond to contemporary values and our

revolutionary life, while remaining open to a whole range of trends and thought from abroad in order to debate what contradicts our culture and to benefit from various elements which are in accordance with our values.
3. Science and its role in our life – educating the individual to make use of rationalism as a means of understanding existence, humanity and society.
4. The sanctification of work and workers.
5. The spread of aesthetic appreciation in all its colours and forms, and from all its sources.
6. A presentation of the benefits of modern civilisation and its problems
7. A struggle against superstition and the frustrating social customs which erode trust.
8. An ongoing call for human rights with relation to freedom, dignity, equality, belief, thought, security and peace.
9. A permanent reminder of the three principles to which our political lives are bound, which are socialism, social peace and national unity.

I do not mean that these principles should be presented as programmes in themselves, but there should be a portrayal of a permanent work ethos which should be alive in the heart of everyone who works in the media and these principles should be discernible in any programme, play, film or game show.

That is what I mean by philosophy. We may differ over one principle or another, and we might suggest adding or removing one, but I hope that we can all agree that the ideal Egyptian is a person who combines the good from his tradition with the good from contemporary culture.

The Right to Arabism

I demand that the Arabs discharge our debts to the last pound, and also that they invest some of their monies in our development plan just as they invest them in Europe and the United States.

How is it that I am brave enough to go public with this demand and in such a forthright manner? It is justifiable for people to demand their rights, rather than demanding support, for are we not people with rights? And what are our rights? And what are our rights when it comes to the Arabs?[1]

I am not claiming rights by dint of the wars we have waged on behalf of the Arab cause. We waged those wars in defence of the homeland we believe to be ours and of a cause we consider our cause. I am not claiming these rights because of the hike in the price of oil as a result of the October War, for we were not fighting for reasons of commerce. We do not resent our brothers' ever-increasing wealth or ask God to give us more and more of it. I am claiming, and demanding, our rightful share on behalf of Arabism, brotherhood, history, the present and the future. What we hope for from these various countries in terms of material unity should be their active contribution to civilisation and modern society.

I do not deny that they have given much aid and many loans. I do not reject what thinking and management lead to. I do not reject the fraternal conferences which have provided help and emergency aid in the most harrowing situations. That is all well known and our gratitude has been expressed, but, in spite of all that, when I consider our situation I find it grim and deplorable. We suffer from a sense of doubting ourselves, and we patiently put up with everything that the bitter race of life unpityingly and unhesitatingly throws at us and suffer through the harsh events that have afflicted our country in its tribulation-laden history. We are a care-worn nation and we strive for even more hardship in order to rescue our country at any cost and no matter what the sacrifice, and no one should be deceived by that small group of us who enjoy excessive wealth. Even if this wealth has affected our calculations and plundered our livelihoods, just like the parasites who appear in times of war and woe in every country, they neither represent a benchmark nor a judgement upon us.

---

1 Although Egyptians are Arab by culture and language, Mahfouz's use of the term here indicates the Arabs with financial clout, i.e., the Saudis and the Gulf Arabs.

And by analogy with these conditions I would say: all the aid or loans offered to us are worth nothing and everything we hear about offered within that framework is worthless. Forgive me for this expression, but it is a sincere expression which states what is truly raging in my heart and in the hearts of millions. We will only be satisfied by a decisive solution, which should not be too much for us – or for you. If what we demand is unreasonable, we apologise unreservedly. If giving us that amount puts a spanner in the works or puts off your cultural rebirth, we will remain apologetically silent, but the situation is not like that. I, and my ilk, have the right to ask each other in confusion and worry about two burdens. If we were asking for a decisive solution from neighbours with whom we have no age-old ties of kinship or everlasting brotherhood, I would say that maybe they like us being weak and in a permanent state of need and are afraid of our strength and the liberation of our will, but what should I say when those neighbours are Arabs and constitute the Arab nation in its everlasting form? And what sort of gift should I demand, for if I apologise would it be a loan to write off our loans which we would then pay off when we achieve a modicum of economic ease? And as for investments, the Arab states are foremost among foreign nations, not including our enemies, and their investments are in line with the Arab economic integration plan which, in my opinion, should be considered the firm base of Arab power, of real unity, and of our desired rebirth.

And yet again I apologise for my forthrightness, but I feel that I am right and in being right in what I demand there is no shame.

20 December 1976

RH

Cultural Aspirations

1. The Relationship between the Arabic Book and the Arab Reader

This is a relationship which has been, or has almost been, completely truncated. There are many obstacles standing in the path of the exporting of Egyptian books to the Arab countries. This is a well known fact and no official has shown real interest in either easing this situation or putting an end to it. It is also difficult for Arabic books to enter the Egyptian market, except for rare cases. It is for this reason that Arab authors are relatively unknown to their audience. What period are we speaking of? The era of space travel, which has shrunk the distances between places and made the world into one large country! It was not the case for Arab authors in the era when books had to be copied by hand, before the invention of the printing press. However, at the beginning of the present century, the Arabs created for themselves a cultural unity with their poets and authors achieving the same degree of recognition from the Atlantic Ocean to the Persian Gulf, a fame enjoyed by both male and female singers and by the nationalist leaders themselves. Today, as I have said, Arab authors, particularly non-Egyptians, are strangers in their own homeland and among their own people. This situation cannot go on being ignored. We live in an age of Arab nationalism when we aim to achieve political and economic unity, and perhaps the solution would be easier if we could agree to establish a distribution company operating on a pan-Arab level with participation from the private and public sectors across the various Arab countries.

2. Defending the Rights of the Author

Copyright is an issue which is supported in some countries, including Egypt, but not yet in the rest of the Arab world. But even in Egypt, in spite of the law having been promulgated in the fifties, it is not applied and the rights of the authors are overlooked in the cinema, the radio and the television, as well as throughout the Arab world. Notwithstanding, there is a class of people which should be encouraged due to their giving their all to write books for a people whose illiteracy rate reaches 70 percent, for there is still a limited proportion of 30 percent of the population who are interested in the written word and are prepared to buy books. It is unarguable that supporting the rights of authors means material and literary encouragement for them. This is something which pushes writers to redouble their efforts at thinking and creating, and creating the necessary cultural climate for a nation trying to advance itself, a nation which became so well known during its periods of enlightenment for encouraging intellectuals and people of taste that it became a byword for that. The protection of authors' rights brings with it a fight against copying and bootleggers. The production of bootleg copies of books is a plague which has spread so much in recent years that it is carried out almost in broad daylight and has been unimaginably deleterious for authors and publishers.

3. Looking After the New Generations

Paying attention to the new generation is paying attention to the future, to the new, to progress, to aspiring for what is better and more beautiful, and is not just being sympathetic to the young and those who rule them. There should be a fair and impartial system in place to spot their talents, to choose the best of them and to smooth their way to employment in the magazine and book publishing industry, and in radio, television and cinema. We should always and forever remember that that is our duty, that it is their right, and that we should do this for the sake of the country and our culture rather than for the sake of any individuals or for a specific generation.

4. Making It Easier to Acquire Books

Book prices have undergone an unreasonable and unacceptable price hike, putting them out of the reach of many consumers, particularly in Egypt. I have here scores or letters complaining about people's inability to acquire books and expressing sincere sorrow over their tangible desire to educate and improve themselves. We need to take a good look at these examples, particularly in our era when many people have moved away from books and towards the cinema, the radio and the television. It is no exaggeration when I say that they are the cream of the students of real culture, but what can we do for them? It might not be the easiest of things at all times to bear material losses in order to make books available, but in these circumstances we have to make them available in large and small bookshops, in cultural institutions and school libraries. This cannot be overlooked or put off.

5. An Arabic Prize

I believe that the time has come to set up a respected prize in the Arab world for science, literature and art, to be awarded to fiction and non-fiction writers who provide laudable services to their countries in particular, and to humanity in general, by dint of their specialisations. Ideally there should also be an annual exhibition in a new Ukaz market. In addition to the encouragement that this prize would offer to the academic and artistic community, it would also direct them towards taking care of their environment which is in the greatest need of their efforts and would free them from having to admire a world which is alien to them – something which sometimes tempts them to favour spurious imitation over real originality.

And last but not least, as they say, I should like ministers of education and culture also to witness the Amman Conference in order to see that culture should be firmly rooted at all stages in schools and to understand that this has an afterlife, whether positive or negative, which does not fade with time.

The Cinema and Notoriety

I should like to speak here of my distress over Egyptian films. By this I mean serious films and serious films alone. I am not ignoring the other films, as those films whose content and form are flops actually pave the way for others to work, provide a livelihood for many and rarely have to overcome obstacles. They rarely face criticism and even more rarely do they face official opposition or protests over their depiction of the nation. A serious film generally represents a foray in thinking as well as an economic adventure. It knows from the outset that it faces unprecedented challenges as it prepares to defend itself against censorship. It fears losing its public in favour of light entertainment films and sometimes includes some spicy elements.

To be perfectly frank, I cannot come up with a defence for this sort of spicing up. It is demoralising and prurient and detracts from the artistic content. It debases sex as an important human force which should be treated, when necessity arises, with seriousness and all due respect, not as a cheap form of stimulation. Art which depends upon this for its success is thereby cheapened. Robust art comes about through thought, expression and rhetoric. My advice to my colleagues in the cinematic world is to avoid sensualisation as part of their role as makers, shakers and pioneers on the road to art and truth. Of no consequence here is the cinematic output of other countries, for every society has its own standards, vision and taste, and it is sufficient for us to study our own technical and intellectual aspects in order to produce some benefit from them without undermining our true originality. I wonder about the role of censorship in doing that and its responsibility for cinematic output. It is an authority that can cleanse any film of its impurities, particularly when done discretely regarding its intellectual content and scenario and then applied to the film as a whole. The law dictates this in order to protect the public on the one hand, and to protect the filmmaker from being exposed to sudden losses on the other. Censorship uses its authentic apparatus, a supreme committee of intellectuals and one of export specialists, and the filmmaker passes through these hurdles and shows his film with a calm mind. But the moment a voice is raised, rightly or wrongly, he finds himself, his film and his money, in the grasp of a new committee and he has to go through the test once again with one difference this time, and that is that he has already spent fifty, sixty or seventy thousand Egyptian pounds! So is it censorship that leads him on to his ruin? And how can he, in this condition, trust the censorship or the Ministry of Culture to which the censorship board is subordinate? Does he need to apply to the United Nations or the Security Council to guarantee his work and money?

That is one side of the argument. The other side is that a serious film looks for criticism from society with regard to the social and human aims it deals with. We are in a state of social unease and in the utmost need of criticism but there are people who advocate it as an urgent and national necessity. However, a critical film faces not inconsiderable obstacles, such as:

1. Protests from the authorities and communities who are the objects of criticism. In the past they have been able to have resort to censorship, and Egyptian films did not find anyone to criticise them, only portraying the 'bad guy' as a two-dimensional ruffian, and for a while films offered nothing more than fantasy or fight scenes. However, the Revolution smashed, amongst other things, the old rods of censorship and opened up a space for positive criticism, among the results of which was the creation of a large number of serious films which portrayed the ugly side of life with the aim of developing and improving it.
2. The delusion of a number of right-minded people is that portraying negative sides of life constitutes an offense against the reputation of society at home and abroad, and that it is our priority to portray what is beautiful or of value as a form of public relations for us and our country. If this logic were correct, we would by analogy need to remove the opposition from parliament for they are believed more than any film, and we would have to rescind the freedom of the press. Moreover, it would perhaps be better to request the police and prosecutor

to ignore delinquents in order to avoid giving ourselves a bad reputation. The truth of the matter is that a trenchant, bold and critical film, by its very art and content, realises the type of good publicity that does not occur to many people. It is a sign of self confidence and a real desire for improvement. It is a sign that it has been made in a free country which reveres freedom and dignity. With regard to the downsides of life that a film might portray, is any country devoid of negative elements? When we watch the new Italian verismo films or the latest American films, we see accusations violently levelled against government, clerics and educators as well as against the judiciary, but these critical portrayals do not tell us about any dark sides of society which do not exist in any other country. They do, however, offer us examples of the intellectual freedom, literary boldness and official tolerance so rarely found except in the developed nations.

3 January 1977
RH

From Top-Down to Bottom-Up

It is not easy to practice a true democratic life in the wake of a dictatorial one that lasted almost a quarter of a century. Government possesses its manner, its vision, and its method, which enter into collective relationships, individual reactions, and every mode of life. A resolution or elections are not enough, nor is a new People's Assembly, to purge the remnants of the old life overnight. What we require is a continuous effort, a firm will, and a true determination, so that we can bring about a new way of thinking and behaving to replace the old one which is to be uprooted. The difficulty of the task is compounded insofar as the dictatorial tendency has its origins in our primitive life, alongside our instincts for violence, aggression, selfishness, and supremacy, whereas the democratic tendency has its origins in rationality. The role of rationality in our life does not compare to that of instinct. Democracy is difficult to foster; it requires a continual fight, unceasing sacrifice, and constant instruction, in order for rationality to take the place of instinct and so that discussion gains ascendency over bigotry, violence, and blind force. I have followed the battles which have broken out in the People's Assembly with interest, pleasure, and optimism. They are a manifestation of health and vitality, the fruit of an unavoidable struggle between primitiveness and rationality, and a genuine effort to purge the old spectres. It is a holy war in which two sides are fighting: the majority and the opposition. Victory will not be achieved by one side or the other; rather, it will be achieved by both, together, over the primitiveness of the dictatorial spirit, which should disappear from the entire arena thanks to the wisdom and patriotism of the two groups.

This is not a call for reconciliation and congeniality. Rather, in reality, it is a call for an increase in struggle and argument on the basis of truth, belief, and nationalism; a call to the majority to exercise its legitimate right to rule, even if this means sometimes opposing the government; a call for the opposition to exercise its legitimate right to dissent on the basis of its principles and aims, even if it supports the government at other times. What we would really like is for the two sides to pledge themselves to rationality and discussion, to pledge themselves to respecting the rights of both the majority and the minority – this is the true, and hoped-for, democratic way. Democracy is a spirit, not forms and words, and the task of the People's Assembly in this regard is to establish the universal dominion of this spirit. To reach the desired goal, I propose cleansing the environment of the following phenomena:

The first is that which some persist in calling 'the dictatorship of the majority'. The truth is that dictatorship will not become a dictatorship unless it rules the majority despotically. As for the majority putting its will into effect, this is its legitimate and democratic right by virtue of it being the majority; it could only become a majority through the will of the people. This startling characterisation was frequently repeated on the occasion of the election of the Assembly's committees and the majority party's insistence on electing members of its party. This is not dictatorship under any circumstances, nor can it be described in this hateful way; rather, it is a policy of some kind which may be deemed right or wrong. However, one cannot have doubts concerning its legitimacy, nor depict it as something other than it is; this would mean that the minority would demand that the majority submits to its view, and this is something which is not compatible with the true democratic spirit.

The second is the lack of an opposition that speaks up or expresses anger. This dereliction can be observed in the Assembly when the authority of those who have the last word to pass judgement in accordance with truth and justice wavers.

The third consists of the sons of the nation whom anger inflamed and who rose up in self-defence. But I will not forgive them their response of inciting those who seek to cause harm and their drift towards destructiveness. In the heat of madness they attacked their achievements which should have been defended against the aggressors and the aberrants. They marred their spontaneous movement and they tarnished it with criminality. They will return to their senses, for they will regret their excesses with regard to themselves and their country.

We need to rethink our entire position by considering events as an inevitable result of intricate factors and not as a result of the economic crisis alone. Among these are:

1. The moral crisis gaining ground in various forms, from corruption in the administration to a lack of regard for values and the law.
2. The general security crisis – this deserves study and analysis. Overt violations, let alone those hatched up in secret, continue to meet no obstacle.
3. The crisis concerning the lack of determination in supervising, following up, and attending to the interests of the people and the state, and what this requires in terms of direction.
4. Respect for democracy, the establishment of its principles, and the issuance of more freedoms.
5. And last but not least, the determination to solve our economic difficulties in a comprehensive and conclusive manner whatever the sacrifices.

The Malady and the Remedy

Everything that can be said to explain the tragedy of Lebanon has been said. It has been said that it is the result of global conspiracies, that it is the result of Arab disputes, that it is the result of the Lebanese system itself which is based upon sectarianism, and that it is the inevitable consequence of the Palestinian presence in Lebanon – and perhaps the tragedy is a result of these factors combined. It really is a dreadful tragedy; it has led to the death of 50,000 people or more, with innumerable people injured, and devastation which has destroyed institutions, buildings, roads, cities, and villages.

If it is true that global powers are responsible, or that they share responsibility, then the leaders, proud in the greatness of their civilisations, deserve a despicable curse upon them which will deprive them of any worthiness with regard to leading mankind. The common expression that small crimes are better than standing up to a giant that is tearing civilisation up at its roots will not excuse the criminal. It is a selfish excuse which ultimately means sacrificing the weak and protecting the strong – there is not one genuine speck of respect for human life in it. If it is true that Arab clashes were responsible for some of the crimes of the tragedy, then for their role they deserve a despicable curse, one more severe and more terrible. It is incumbent upon the Arabs to reconsider what they are in dispute about, to discuss their differences in a friendly manner, or behave, during their disagreement, in a disciplined manner and remain within the bounds of humaneness when anger pushes them to overstep the bounds of brotherhood.

If it is true that the sectarianism enshrined in Lebanon is responsible for the tragedy, then I hope that the martyred souls will decisively persuade them of the weakness of sectarianism as a fragile basis for a nation, and that there is no substitute for citizenship as a bond for citizens in which the sects and religions dissolve and join together in brotherhood, peace, and equality.

If it is true that the poor distribution of wealth is responsible, or partially responsible, for the tragedy, then the incontrovertible truth is that there will be no peace, stability, progress, and security for a country whose system is based upon exploitation, and that social justice is indispensible in this era which has been known as the era of the ordinary people.

And if it is true that the Palestinian presence is among the factors responsible for the tragedy, then I hope that things proceed according to the wisdom that will preserve the sovereignty of the host country, and that the security of the Palestinians will be safeguarded until they return to their homeland at the nearest opportunity, God willing.

Whatever the case may be, if the Lebanese structure were not built on a fragile foundation, then, under no circumstances, would it be exposed to the cunning of deceivers or the plots of dissenters.

Therefore, there is no escaping the destruction of the old foundation and the construction of a new, solid foundation that is worthy of a people upon whom God has bestowed intelligence, energy, and ability. I call on every Arab to follow what is happening in Lebanon, to witness the birth of the happy solution where the wounds of the past, and its shortcomings, are bandaged up. I call upon every Arab because Lebanon is not the only country which has suffered from its negative aspects and its shortcomings. Lebanon is merely an illustration upon whose page flaws – which are possessed by other Arab countries to varying degrees – have come to the fore. Sectarianism, confessional prejudices, and despotism, are deficiencies which were not at one time restricted to Lebanon alone. The tragedy burst forth in Lebanon as a warning to all who are heedless, indifferent, and ignorant. We hope that the wisdom of the Lebanese will produce a wise and successful solution by which they will cure their wounds and, at the same time, which will promote a common remedy for any sensible person who wants to benefit from it in our Arab homeland.

17 January 1977

AB

Complaints as a Prelude to Administrative Reform

These days there have been discussions about complaints and censorship in the Suggestions and Complaints Committee of the parliament, and I believe that behind this there is a real desire to see the wrongs of the people redressed and a noble wish to see administrative reform. There may appear to be no meaningful connection between these two aims, but they are actually indivisible.

That is because every credible complaint alludes to the flaws in some apparatus of the state and if a complaint receives the necessary attention, and if the grounds are treated with good will and resoluteness, more than one aim is achieved. On the one hand, this relieves a citizen's suffering – this is an aim in and of itself, but it also gives the citizen a sense of attachment to a government which is not deaf to his cries. On the other hand, it also eradicates a flaw, a lack of concern or even negligence on the part of the apparatus being complained about, and makes the people who work there feel that there is a watchful eye over them, that there is accountability and that the administration is working properly.

The investigation of a few hundred complaints might well bring about a miracle in the working practices of the administration and kick-start it which is an aim for which we designated a whole year which we called the Year of Administrative Revolution. It started off with fine words and ended with fine words because we concentrated on the regulations and bureaucracy as the two main factors mitigating against human activity.

So let us remind those interested parties that complaints are a singular prelude not only to redressing the wrongs suffered by the people but that the Egyptian bureaucracy has become mired in its own ways and its working practices have become an impediment to people's hopes.

24 April 1980

RH

A Word on Sedition

I have this to say to the investigative commission dealing with sectarian sedition:

1. The sedition is not sectarian; rather, it is national. The members of the commission are called upon in their capacity as Egyptians to investigate its contingent causes and remedy it by means of the eternal national spirit.
2. Though it is harming the safety of the Copts, it is more severely harming the honour of the Muslims, a religion of humane morals and values which has been passed down over generations. It is your duty to prevent one group from harm and the other group from committing sin.
3. Sirs, know that there can be no successful remedy prior to an accurate diagnosis.
4. Know also that the Copts are not the victims of the Muslims; rather, the Copts and the Muslims are the victims of a third power.
5. Is the third power an aberrant religious current? And how is it possible that it become aberrant in a country in which the richest citizens follow the example of the religious scholars? Or is it that the Copts, the Muslims, and the aberrant religious current, are victims of a fourth power, or an oppressive pathological condition?

I ask God, the munificent, for your right action and success.

27 April 1980
AB

Arabs and Arabism

We dilly and dally, we mouth slogans, we continue to take initiatives, and we address the various peoples. These are the alternatives on offer to define our position with regard to the Arabs and Arabism. We have to differentiate between the Arabs and Arabism just as we differentiate between a historical period and the whole of history, between the start of something and its further development. The Arabs of our era have had their disputes with us and we have had ours with them. We have come together and we both speak in the name of Arabism, but this should not allow us to forget the original and root cause of the dispute. Therefore, it is unavoidable that we should:

1. Continue with initiatives without indecision or hesitation.
2. Desist on our part from quarrelling with Arab governments, ignore what they say about us and their subjective radio broadcasts.
3. Welcome any serious effort to solve the problem on their part and offer it our full support.
4. Continue addressing the Arabs regarding what has brought us together from olden times and will do so forever more, such as history, heritage, culture, art and common concerns. Therein, we have an unstoppable vehicle which is the Voice of the Arabs,[1] and this should be the voice of certainty and truth amid

1 Voice of the Arabs was a radio station which broadcast from Cairo starting from 1953. It was an equivalent of the BBC World Service, and generally had an agenda of pan-Arabism, Arab unity and socialism.

> all the hubbub. It should provide intelligent news and discussion and allow conversations on a range of subjects outside the field of politics. It should offer programmes on culture and philosophy by making a monthly programme on authors from Arab countries presented within the context of educated Arabism and avoiding any form of incitement.

Thereafter, we must accept any hand which is stretched out to us whether by the moderate or the rejectionist states.[2] That way we will live up to our full responsibility.

1 May 1980
RH

2 The division of the Arab states into moderate and rejectionist is based upon whether a state accepted that Israel should exist in some form or other.

Genies and the Intellect

The existence of genies has had such a significant effect on our way of thinking that we give them equal importance alongside our local and international concerns. It is taken for granted that there are living creatures with us in this world, who are perhaps intelligent as well but about whom we know nothing. They can make contact with us and we might contact them one day. There is a way of getting to know them and that is through conjecture; we use that, perhaps, as our path to truths which cannot be submitted to rational proof. Rationality is the best thing we have for dealing with reality – the reality of nature and of society. It is the real force behind human achievements in science and culture which range from our daily life to space exploration. We should remember that when we revise the teaching syllabus, manage public relations or speak to the public from some soapbox or other. We should remember that around 70 percent of our population are illiterate and that they are a people with a superstition-riddled culture that they make conform with the rigours of contemporary life. We should remember that the evil brought about by superstition is no less dangerous than that of hunger, ignorance or disease. Is it not strange that the nation should be so sensitised to the chimera of a cultural invasion but that we pay no heed to the damaging invasion of irrational beliefs?

4 May 1980

RH

Aberration

I would like to make a distinction between extremism and aberration. Extremism represents the achievement of the utmost degree of faith with regard to any doctrine of belief. The fighting elite belong to it; it is founded upon knowledge and morality, and always ready to give, and to sacrifice itself for the sake of the highest ideal. As for aberration, it exceeds the proper bounds due to the pressure of a reckless emotion which is based upon ignorance; it is driven by delusion and plunges headlong towards harm and aggression.

I am asking what is responsible for aberration. People's opinions veer toward this or that, but the truth is that we are all responsible for it insofar as we are responsible for the prevailing corruption and the climate of malaise which form a wall of evil that produces aberration as a reaction to it. Therefore, the remedy will be found when there is genuine and universal opposition toward corruption, when there is true religious education and preachers whose hearts are filled with the love of God and man, when the fragrance of a certain freedom pervades the air – one which grants young people choice, debate, and self-realisation in the light of day – and when we present a good example in a difficult time.

22 May 1980

AB

Oversight and Administration, Accountability and Reward

On the occasion of the establishment of a complaints procedure, I recall the field visits paid by the censorship administration to the telephone exchanges of Cairo and the shortcomings they found there which were included in their report to the minister of telecommunications accompanied by their evaluation of the exchange directors. I return to the subject of the administration, because of its remit to operate with delicacy and good faith, for the general welfare of the country is the point of hope for containing the crisis, for carrying out the five-year development plan, and for making cultural advances.

The basis of this remit is that it should come from within, but the country cannot wait until the citizen is completely reformed, and the only active means we have are those of monitoring and determination. We have the apparatus of administrative oversight, but perhaps in the prevailing circumstances this does not satisfy our striving for perfection; it needs extra manpower and how much underemployment we have in the civil service! The oversight department could extend its specialisations and stipulate that its recommendations be carried out; it could work in collaboration with the complaints administrations and draw up a general policy for field visits, for putting an end to sloppiness and laxity in the fields of telecommunications, subsidies and inoperative laws, etc., etc.

There must also be accountability as well as some form of incentive so that good working practices will trickle down and then back up again. Any general manager will be the first to be asked why there are so many complaints against the organisation he heads, why there are still shortcomings in its services, what the policy is regarding the management of his organisation, and how he supervises his subordinates and serves the people. A general manager will then remain in his position, be transferred back to the Ministry, or pensioned off according to his degree of concern and aptitude. That will all come about if we strive for success with the seriousness that this matter deserves.

29 May 1980

RH

Universities and the Responsibility of Criticism

Does criticism apply to some people and not to others? In order to deflect this question, criticism itself should be a natural state of activity, and if a critic stops producing criticism, it is useless for us to ask why he is either interested or not.

If we were to sketch out the geography of criticism, we would see it in this manner: our movement at the outset of our national rebirth was generally restricted to pure criticism, just as criticism at the start of the 1950s fell victim to positivism. The turn of the 20th century was characterised by tangible works of criticism, and by trends which dealt critically with Egypt's cultural history and with contemporary and Western literature. Thanks to all of this we have come to know much about the critical movements in our history which still affect contemporary authors including Ahmed Shawqi,[1] al-Rafi'i,[2] el-Akkad,[3] and Taha Hussein.[4] Then, in the 1940s, creativity took over and criticism was more or less relegated to the back burner. I believe that criticism came back as a movement between the fifties and sixties and in the period following it up until the catastrophe of

---

1 Ahmed Shawqi (1868–1932), poet and dramatist.

2 Mustafa Sadiq al-Rafi'i (1880–1937), writer of prose and literary conservative.

3 Abbas el-Akkad (1889–1964), journalist, poet and literary critic.

4 Taha Hussein (1889–1973), author, intellectual and leader of the Egyptian Renaissance.

1967 after which there was a period of stasis in both criticism and creativity.

And now we come to a remark which I cannot leave out here: during the years when criticism was active nothing fell outside its remit. The proof of that is that great quantities of criticism were published on poetry by the likes of Ahmed Shawqi, on prose by al-Manfaluti,[5] el-Akkad, al-Rafi'i and Tawfiq al-Hakim,[6] constituting an important critical movement which marked Arabic thought.

In truth, we cannot be absolutely certain that criticism overlooked anyone but we can hold it responsible for two important flaws:

1. The slowness in discovering new talents.
2. A concentration on leading personalities.

In our culture, as we all know, criticism deals with the high points of culture – as if this is the only thing which deserves endeavour. That is the only section of literature that the reader keeps being referred to, with the result being that up-and-coming contemporary authors are overlooked. We can add to this the fact that political criticism consequently became obsequious and led to the emergence of literary power centres. The trend of criticism became somewhat similar to memoranda written between a government secretary and his manager. This is unfortunately a fair depiction of literary criticism.

When it comes to real criticism, it must first of all deal with the discovery of new talents and level criticism against contemporary authors no matter the rank or school of writing. Any call for writing of the theory of our literary and intellectual history will bear no fruit – I believe, and am almost certain, that the universities are responsible for this. Although it is the universities' job to produce Masters and PhD treatises, there are still many people who deserve an education and whom we have overlooked.

The role of the university in our intellectual life is to provide creative

---

5 Mustafa Lutfi el-Manfaluti (1876–1924), author and poet.

6 Tawfiq al-Hakim (1898–1987), novelist and dramatist.

leadership so that, through its academic systems and pedagogy, it can identify phenomena and examine literary issues.

15 July 1980

RH

Islamic Experiments

Contemporary Islamic thought is replete with many currents ranging from the intensely conservative to the boldly progressive. In many instances thinking has gone beyond the sphere of theory to that of application and testing, resulting in various experiments taking place in Iran, Pakistan, Saudi Arabia, Egypt, and Turkey. These include the salafist, the revolutionary, the moderate, and the secular. Each system approaches life with its intellectual elements and its theological rulings, occupied with the challenges of contemporary life and strongly determined to achieve reconciliation and success. Success will be decided for this movement or that one according to the results it achieves and the problems that it solves. I believe that the one which is successful will be the one which predominates and spreads, and that it will only succeed, predominate, and spread on certain conditions. Among these is that it demonstrates that it is suitable for contemporary life and better able to solve its problems, that it actualises social justice and both individual and social freedom, that it respects – in both word and deed – the rights of man, and in this way solves, humanely and decisively, the problems of religious, racial, and ethnic minorities. All of this will be accomplished through the framework of eternal, sublime values and the noble, optimistic life.

14 August 1980

AB

Until They Change What Is in Themselves

In recalling our recent past, we lament the two great failures that befell us: the failure of democracy prior to the July Revolution and the failure of the socialist experiment in the first phase of the July Revolution. We seek causes for the failure. We look for them in the things that surround us: in colonialism, the monarchy, and the parties prior to the revolution, in international Zionism, and in domestic and foreign conspiracies following the revolution. There may be some truth to this, but it is not the whole truth. There is the principal responsibility which the people bear, there are the responses of individuals and the negative attitudes they contain with regard to the will to work and create, and the degree of dedication regarding the public interest. The culpability does not lie with colonialism and the monarchy alone. It lies with the important men who were enticed by temptation and blinded by the love of power. It lies with the people who did not get angry with the intensity required, just as it lies with the men who were deceived by greed; they embarked on the socialist experiment intent on pillage and spoliation, and they dreamed prematurely of imperial greatness. Truly, we have undergone two big lessons which confirm, always and forever, that any experiment for progress – irrespective of whether the conditions are favourable or adverse – depends, first and foremost, upon the men of importance, upon dedication, truthfulness, integrity, and belief. 'Indeed, God will not change the condition of a people until they change what is in themselves.'[1]

28 August 1980
AB

1 This quotation is an excerpt from the Qur'an 13:11.

The Long-Awaited Revolution

When man discovered modern science, the door to the previously unknown opened for humanity, with the only way to gain an understanding of that being through various specialisations. With the resultant technological progress humanity, for reasons of power and control, has been able to achieve things we had not even dreamt about. Success in these two fields came about not only as the fruit of intellectual collaboration between the advanced and progressive states, but as the fruit of the human endeavour in which mankind has participated since its first existence and of man's creative striving for eternity. That is why science is characterised by a global character and its universality has given rise to many hopes. However, sometimes for reasons to do with national security, and sometimes for reasons to do with the economy, many research centres and laboratories have been forced to operate in secrecy, and this has often prevented them from fruitful intellectual collaboration or from benefitting from other achievements. We should remember that just as much effort has been spent in various fields to come up with hellish methods of ending civilisation and destroying every last human. It is for this reason that there has arisen a dangerous contradiction between worldwide human endeavour in its very nature and the self-serving aims and interests of various nationalisms. And this is how politicians who represent short-term interests have managed to control those intellectuals qualified to lead humanity towards lofty and distant aims. It is as if the world today awaits a revolution of a new type, a revolution by intellectuals against politicians, a revolution which places academic values above commercial ones, a revolution which will give liberation and freedom a new meaning and a new redemption

4 September 1980
RH

Hollow Slogans

Between content and form there is a fine relationship based on complete equilibrium. The content should not outweigh the form and the form should not outbalance the content. This law does not just apply to art but wherever there is a question of content and form in the various types of social and human activity such as the economy, politics and religion, etc. The form can only be dictated by the content and the essence, the conclusive result of that being the spirit becoming more important than the letter, the diminution of the essence in favour of the visible, and the depths of a meaning being subordinate to the superficial. Take religion, for example, and you will find that it has many functions including addressing the heart and the intellect, but, in many cases, it has been reduced to a discussion about how to perform the religious ablutions, or what constitutes breaking one's fast, or the exact time at which a festival should start. I do not mean that these are not matters of importance, but I should like them to have a sense of proportionality. We have read about a group in some Muslim countries which has taken upon itself to be guardians of the public morals, and we have read how they turn latecomers away from prayers at the mosque and similar things, but we have not heard their opinions about the money squandered in nightclubs in various capital cities, or about respect for the principle of consultation in the political system of their country, or the principle of inclusion in their economic system.[1] The simple mouthing of slogans does not deceive me but I examine them in

1 Mahfouz is taking aim, here, at the ultra-conservative Wahhabis in Saudi Arabia.

the light of the issue of form and content, and I remember that sometimes a flare-up of enthusiasm serves to camouflage secret feelings of guilt and impotence.

11 September 1980
RH

The Voice That Must Be Heard

In confronting extremism, and as a response to it, another voice has spoken up: the voice of rationality and secularism. It is nothing new in our contemporary life; however, its speaking up at this time has been accompanied by an extraordinary moral courage which attests the sincerity, good faith, and sense of responsibility of those who have raised this voice. At base it harbours no hostility towards religion, but seeks a separation between religion and politics, and seeks to liberate the will in the face of contemporary problems. There is no doubt that it is an unfabricated truth, inasmuch as it expresses a sizable, existing current. However, as a remedy for extremism it should be considered ineffective, in my opinion. It is preposterous that a youth would be snatched away from the current of extremism and then embrace that which stands accused of apostasy and enmity towards religion by the other side. The situation is made more difficult by enemies of religion who infiltrate it and whose pens flow with words of incitement apt for compounding the impetuousness of extremism instead of rocking it to sleep. No, this is not the desired remedy. Perhaps the remedy is to be found in true Islam, as that called for by a community which recognises both faith and enlightenment together, which is dedicated to timeless values, whose dedication is to the age and to progress, and which sees in Islam a spirit which lends itself to every time and place. If it utilises its valuable means of diligence, rationality, and its breadth of horizons, I do not find in this thinking anything that threatens the safety of the community in the march of its progress, the system of its governance, its economy, its national unity, and respect for the humanity of women.

Indeed, it promises to traverse the straight path towards modern civilisation supported by values which may be missing in Western civilisation itself at present. It can fill the nation's youth with a new vigour that will incline them towards a true sense of membership and give them energy to work, create, and achieve. This is the thinking which will cultivate a basis for discourse, advocacy, and education. We must give this enlightened community of believers control over religious education in schools, mosques, and the media; it is the voice of Islam, the Islam of reason, compassion, justice, and civilisation.

18 September 1980

AB

Negative Aspects of Society and Things That Shouldn't Be Done!

Cinema and television are being subjected to campaigns of harsh criticism for having depicted negative aspects of society – something which the critics consider tantamount to defamation of the country and its population, and which the censor should clamp down on. We need to differentiate between serious art that deals with subjects seriously – and when necessary, with grave humanitarian and social phenomena such as criminality and sex – and commercial output which deals with these phenomena in a sensationalist or lurid manner. A society that sincerely and resolutely seeks improvement does not fear criticism and does not seek to cover up the unmentionable, but considers portraying this and laying bare the negative aspects of society as a salubrious and active means of improving and purifying society. That is why they should be encouraged and respected, and the freedom to criticise should be defended. Art, in the final analysis, is culture, and not propaganda or public relations, and exposing the dark side of society can only harm those who profit from it or actively participate in it. Furthermore, those striving for corrective measures are harmed by keeping these things covered up and the avoidance of confronting them. Art cannot be harmed by scrutiny, whether from close or afar, by a friend or an enemy, if the programme and filmmakers believe in themselves and attempt to portray on screen the truth, rather than a sanitised version of society.

16 October 1980

RH

From the Multitude to the Society

Not every human multitude is a society; society is a phenomenon more advanced than the multitude, by generations and phases. In my view, a society does not deserve its name unless it meets important, necessary conditions. Among these are that it does not lack a goal, or several goals, which will achieve supremacy over any era of its history, and that the goals will encompass its individuals, in a general way, and bring them together. Another condition is that a mutual trust exists among the people on one hand, and the governing apparatus on the other, based upon honesty and mutual respect, even if expectations are realised slowly and with difficulty. A further condition is that human rights are to be respected within it; there should be no violation against dignity, thought must not be suppressed, inclination must not be impeded, the weak should not be degraded, the strong should not prevail, the majority should not have a monopoly, and a minority should not be harmed. Furthermore, privileges of class, family, and bureaucracy must be eradicated, and destinies should be determined under the protection of a just law and humane customs. Our revolutions have occurred successively, endeavouring towards this aim, that is to say, in order to remove us from the darkness of the multitude and move us toward the light of the purposeful, contemporary, humane society. Though, from time to time, we ought to recall past sacrifices and noble goals.

23 October 1980

AB

Culture and the Broadcast Media

Popular and mass culture has had, and still has, great success in both forms of the media: the aural and the visual. High culture has also met with success within the framework of television's Second Programme and some other television programmes. In times gone by we did not demand that the Second Programme's signal be strengthened so that it could be heard not just the length and breadth of our republic but in the Arab countries, if possible. However, today we should demand more than that given the state of stagnation of cultural and intellectual activity with so many people enumerating the reasons for that. We should demand more as the administration of the whole cultural apparatus in the state has now been reformed, with educated observers of differing views and trends calling for the right conditions to be created to allow for a flourishing of thought and creativity. That is why the broadcast media, in both its forms, must take on more of the burden in this domain. It must transform itself into a cultural flagship inasmuch as it is the media flagship in the struggle for hearts and minds. I confess to being grateful for the sincere effort and conscious perseverance now being expended in the service of culture, but I hope for a redoubling of such vigour and awareness. It should be remembered that this will be for the benefit of decent people everywhere.

30 October 1980

RH

The Muslims between Muhammad (Peace Be upon Him) and Abu Lahab

Congratulations to the Muslim world on the occasion of the Islamic New Year. It is deserving of congratulation for the glory of the anniversary on one hand, and for this spiritual awakening which is bursting forth within its vast tracts, announcing a new resurgence, on the other. Besides this, perhaps it is deserving of lamentation and consolation due to the crimes committed upon its soil which defy its principles and transgress its moral codes. It charged its sons with brotherhood and love, yet see them fighting with one another as hostile nations and fighting one another within the single homeland as sects and tribes.

Islam commanded them to consult, yet see their rulers govern them despotically with the highhandedness of invaders towards prisoners of war. It charged them with solidarity and justice, yet see how the rich among them exploit the poor and how the greed of the powerful, with their privileges, has broken them. It urged them toward knowledge and cleanliness, yet see the ignorance and sickness ravaging the vast majority. It exalted human rights, yet we see those with knowledge and convictions in the company of those following criminal pursuits. It ordered them to respect the rights of those different from them in religion, yet see the intriguer picking quarrels in their regions. Indeed, it reveals a sad picture; it shows that a great number of Muslims are devoted to Abu Lahab – a greater number than those who are devoted to Muhammad ibn 'Abdullah (peace and blessings be upon him).[1]

---

1 Muhammad ibn 'Abullah refers to the Prophet Muhammad. The latter part is his

However, the Messenger of God has taught us not to give up in the face of despair, that the night – no matter how looming – has an end, and that the sun shall rise on the morrow.

6 November 1980
AB

patronymic, meaning 'son of 'Abdullah'. Abu Lahab was Muhammad's paternal uncle and is chiefly remembered for his enmity toward Islam and his persecution of the prophet.

A Decision of the Majority Party

Some newspapers reported that the National Party, in its discussion of the new housing law, did not agree to raising the rates paid by the residents of old buildings, so as to avoid increasing their burdens in their current living conditions. This kind of decision testifies, more so than any referendum or election, that the party represents the majority of the people. The party was elected in light of principles which it proclaimed prior to diving into the waves of action and practice. As for this decision and its like, it demonstrates that it is a party which is not separate from the popular base to the rhythm of whose agonies and hopes it pulses, and you will not find a more accurate definition for a party of the majority than that, at any time or in any place. The decision also demonstrates that it fully accords with most of the principles advocated by the state, which it imposes as a duty for any party seeking public service, such as socialism and social peace. Perhaps it is very necessary, with regard to any bill or resolution, that we turn to our principles set out in the constitution so that congruence is achieved between word and deed, between intention and practice, and between the basis on which we conducted the referenda and that which we apply to the individual and the collective.

20 November 1980

AB

Between Opinion and Action

With the formation of the Shura Council our advisory institutions have grown in number to an extent which they have not in other countries.[1] We have national councils that are specialised in terms of their members, who are the most knowledgeable in various branches of human activity and who are working towards both long-term and short-term goals. Behold the Shura Council with its members elected from people of opinion and knowledge, and whose views the state will make use of when circumstances require a pertinent opinion and mindful knowledge. These opinions gather finally in the hands of the People's Assembly. This is the principal legislative power and the representative of the people in all their types – peasants, workers, and the upper classes – in light of whom it makes its final decisions. Here we recall those other people of opinion and knowledge who spoke up every week, or every month, in the opposition newspapers and, thereby, gave a complete illustration of opinion and counsel. However, opinion and counsel are not everything; indeed, they are nothing unless they are coupled with implementation and action. For the form of action to be fulfilled, like the form of opinion, we must take a learned interest in considering the utilisation of our human wealth, in placing the worker in his appropriate position, and in linking wages with production, just as we take an interest in monitoring and tracking,

1 The term 'shura' (*shūrā*) in Arabic means 'advice' or 'consultation'. The Shura Council was the upper house of the Parliament of Egypt. It was created in 1980 and dissolved in 2013.

and encouraging the industrious and deterring those who are negligent. We are in a predicament and we will only get out of it by mobilising the forces and unleashing the energies in a clean atmosphere right for sacrifice and giving.

27 November 1980
AB

A Basic Principle in the Case of Graduates

At long last the case of jobs for graduates is being subjected to study and rationalisation. This should have been done before the decision was taken on a country-wide basis to make the employment of graduates obligatory. The matter should have been considered an integral part of the issue of education, educational reform and development in general. In saying this, I do not intend to go over the whole matter thoroughly as I have already done that time and time again over the last few years, but I want to bring the attention of the researchers to a general principle that must be the basis of any administrative decrees regarding the appointment and distribution of graduates across the country. It is a principle based on clarity, precision, justice and integrity whereby every graduate should know his fate in light of his specialisation and efforts, without any exception or favouritism. There should be no loopholes through which nepotism or opportunism can creep, and no distinction of class, party or family. We will achieve a high level of intellectual activity by remaining mindful of our responsibility and by gaining the trust of the people in general. People and the rising generations will feel reassured; we will remove the spectre of betrayal from the rights of the population and, at the same time, we will nurture social peace and national unity.

4 December 1980

RH

Our Fate Lies in the Hands of the Labour Force

In our current conditions, in our difficult and complicated circumstances, as we cleave a path towards development and rebirth, the thing in desperate need of a core value is work. Our hope for salvation is based on work and the degree of success or failure is in direct proportion to the amount of energy we expend on work. Our bodily, intellectual and spiritual nourishment can only be satisfied through work. That is why we must ponder night and day how we can impel our latent strengths to work harder, better, and with more continuity, by considering work to be our primary objective. How can we get people to believe in work? How do we recompense them for it? How should we deal with the negligent, the lazy and the errant?

Let us turn our attention to the workforce for that is the basis of work. Their preparation starts in primary school when children receive their moral education, educational preparation and training, when they are directed towards various special subjects according to their educational abilities, and which are based on the needs of the state education plan and those of the Arab and African region. We should also take another look at sending workers around the country to places where there are employment opportunities. As you can see, the issue is not limited to graduates alone, but it is one of our policy towards manpower in the light of the requirements of this difficult period, and in the shadow of rational planning and comprehensive national justice.

11 December 1980

RH

The Great People of History Series

Before going on to make another series about the greatest men and women, we must define the purpose of this series. Is it to do with presenting an artistic portrayal of them, or is it about providing a complete picture of their characters backed up by moral, psychological and historical truths? Or is it supposed to highlight the positive roles they have played in our lives? Naturally, each of these aims necessitates special treatment. If an artistic portrayal is the aim, then the imagination has its role to play and the entertainment and thrill element may sometimes supersede pure fact. If an honest portrayal is the purpose, then there is no escape from presenting the truth in all its positive and negative aspects. If the purpose is to highlight their positive role, perhaps the best way to do so is in a biopic or a serialisation with a sound academic and historical basis which takes pains to show their struggle, their way of thinking and the historical circumstances which they endured. It is my belief that an artistic portrayal might give those unfamiliar with these characters a skewed version, but that an honest portrayal might come into conflict with the traditions of our society and come across as wilfully offensive. The only way is to highlight their positive role in a truthful manner, one which acknowledges their success and sends out a renewed message to those in power and which provides patriotic educational value for our children and grandchildren. I say all this on the occasion of the broadcast of the Great People of History series which vacillates between fact and fiction, between respectful depiction and offense. The opportunity to exploit this in a better manner has been wasted.

25 December 1980

RH

Deeds and Men

In our lifetimes, we can witness great achievements by people who are highly motivated, whose consciences are sincere and who are devoted to their work, just as we have witnessed palpable benefits in various fields which lead us along the path of development, construction and hope. These include our first budget surplus since time immemorial which has provided a welcome drop of sweet water for our parched mouths. These also include the completion of the bypasses in the Suez Canal to enable its use by super tankers which is a great achievement and deserving of a people known over the course of history for their patience, perseverance and construction skills, as well as being a living testimony to their great work efficiency and outstanding managerial skills.

These achievements also include the new system of teaching and a new clearing system for matching students with universities – which will be put into operation next year. It is a new Corrective Revolution which is being carried out with wisdom and calm in the field of education and we should engrave its starting date in our history to commemorate a significant and exhilarating event. It is a revolution which aims at building up the Egyptian citizen and equipping him with the values and knowledge he needs to face modern life in all its complications. These are examples of the deeds and the men who have made themselves a role model for anyone who believes in his God, his homeland, his brother and humankind.

8 January 1981

RH

Diagnosing Calamity

It is one of our bad habits that, if a calamity comes upon us, we rush to diagnose it without any vision and we accuse bad luck, fate, our opponents or world imperialism, taking ourselves out of the picture completely, as if we are no more than the innocent victims of one of those causes – or all of them together. I would like to suggest a cure for this dire habit which is that we should start off by diagnosing the calamity with reference to ourselves first. Perhaps we have thought something through badly, acted badly or something in our planning is responsible for the state we are in, in addition to taking into account bad luck, fate, our opponents or world imperialism. Obviously I am not suggesting this purely for the sake of theorising but for the practical purpose of being able to change our fate ourselves. Here is an example of what I mean: the famous Arab situation of no war, no peace. I am not saying anything new if I state that any dispute between countries can be resolved in one of two ways, either by war or by negotiation. But we have created a third solution, which is not a solution, which is no war, no peace. If summoned to war, people say the time is not right yet, and if summoned to negotiation, people scream about betrayal, surrender and defeat. So, the only situation left is one of no war, no peace, in other words, what is really a period of preparation until the opportunity presents itself and we have the power to overcome our opponents, but what opponent would simply wait idly by until fate brings this about? The inevitable outcome, therefore, is that the opponent will wage a preventative war for the flimsiest of reasons, or even without a reason claiming that it is a war of defence, and you will always find people who believe the enemy and back him up. That is how we have ended up going through war after war followed by losses, and we carry on cursing our bad luck, our fate, our adversary or world imperialism. The thing which deserves our opprobrium is actually our way of seeing things and our actions, as well as the arms dealers around the world who are the first to profit from our obduracy.

1 February 1981
RH

People Deserving Pity

The press is a faithful mirror of the concerns of people on both the local and the global level. Hence, sensationalising a piece of news to grab people's attention or underplaying it is an important social, psychological and ethical marker. Accordingly, the demise of one of the Beatles took up large amounts of column inches in the world press, and it was the same with the earlier defeat of Clay,[1] as is the case for daily tittle-tattle to do with the divorce of some artiste, or some other celebrity embarking on a new affair. We have no objection to the masses being interested in sport, light music, or beauties of every type and species, but I am amazed that the news item about the year-on-year deaths of 13 million infants due to poverty is hidden away somewhere on the inside pages of the newspaper, in barely legible type and without any comment! We are not living in the year 10,000 BCE but in 1981 which is a whole quarter century after the conquest of space. The news report appeared next to a piece on the amounts spent annually on armaments which is now 15 billion dollars every 15 days! What does that say about human civilisation in the last quarter of the twentieth century? I am not saying that civilisation is disintegrating or decadent, but I am saying that in spite of the enormous and dazzling achievements in various fields of human endeavour, these have not managed to create a human conscience, or any strength or practicality, and, hence, we should lament the state of humanity in general. These

1 That is, Cassius Clay, the boxer better known as Muhammad Ali (1942–2016).

achievements are a sign of what is bad in the world, although they could also be a sign of what is good.

13 February 1981

RH

A Difficult Transitional Period

They speak bitterly to you about the flops in the theatre and film world these days. They ascribe this to the vagaries of the masses as a result of their suddenly finding a surplus of foodstuffs available. As if those complaining have to cope with thespian flops and a glut of food at the same time, but their irony is not devoid of resentment and protest. With regard to foodstuffs, it is perhaps the positive effect of the first Infitah,[1] which, despite its strong need for reform and rationalisation, raised the level of sections of the population, the austerity of whose lives had hardly been touched over the course of our long history. These were groups which knew only continuous graft and food scarcity. We should be happy for what they have achieved and help them to gain more. We should not consider their influence on theatre and cinema to be that of unmitigated evil or of an incurable disease. If nothing else, during this transitional period, this has made the stage and cinema both sit up and take notice of what people do with their free time. The cultural level will catch up with the material level at some point in the near future, and this will doubtless have an effect on improving the popular arts as well as serious art which is in such a parlous state at the moment, and a not insignificant number of people will earn a livelihood from that. Having said all of this, I would add that the poor bear no responsibility for the parlous state of serious theatre and the cinema, for these two institutions' problems go back generally to the hardships caused by

1 The Infitah was a programme instituted by Anwar Sadat to 'open the door' and liberalise the economy in the years following the 1973 October War.

the economic crisis. Now people prefer to stay away from traffic jams, to sit in front of their television sets and to spend their money on life's necessities. This is perhaps a difficult and bumpy transitional period but some sense of balance will return if God wills it.

19 February 1981
RH

The Meaning of Science and Faith

Among the run-of-the-mill news items that are published in our newspapers in such a way that they do not catch the eye, I read that Egyptian scientists have hit upon a design for a new device for producing energy from village waste. Its costs – on account of local, raw materials – reached approximately 500 Egyptian pounds and tests verified the capability of obtaining energy from biogas equal to six times that of energy generated from solid fuels through conventional methods. The news item and the manner of its publication reminded me of the dark, quiet atmosphere that our scientists work in without material or moral recompense. Likewise, it reminded me of the problem of brain drain – from time to time we have snivelled over it, though we are responsible for it first and foremost. It also reminded me of another migration: the movement of scientists from their original field to that of religion, using their learning in the interpretation of the Noble Qur'an, and in the composition of doctrine and Islamic law. Perhaps they think that they are bringing science and faith together. The truth is that many religious people object to this approach both in terms of form and substance. As a matter of fact, the import of science and faith is not, in my view, that we employ science to explain religion, but that we take from faith a strength which will support us in the labour of scientific research, in the discovery of its secrets, and in the creation of its inventions, as a service to the nation and to humanity. The scientist who is a believer is, in truth, not the one who leaves the institute in order to interpret the Qur'an; rather, he is the one who consecrates his life to science, research, and to man.

22 February 1981

AB

What Do We Want from the Shura Council?

It is well known that the principle aim of the Shura Council is to preserve the heritage of the July Revolution, and that of May 15. Some may view the expansion of its sphere of activity as the next step, while others hope that it will turn into a senate. However, in all cases it must remain connected, in the consciousness of the people, with this revolutionary aim which granted it the right to exist, that is, to preserve the heritage of the Revolution.

The truth is that the advisory apparatuses are not few. Among them is one which works towards the long term, such as the National Council, and one which is faced with the demands of political and social life hour by hour, such as the People's Assembly. However, the burdens are many, the aspirations are high, and disagreements are not uncommon – perhaps values are forgotten in the throng of activity which should not be forgotten. Because of this, it is necessary that the hopes of the people are connected to the Shura Council as the strong line of defence for their revolutionary spirit, for the gains of their just struggle, and their hopes for a better tomorrow. Certainly, it is important, in itself, that the Council voices its opinion and strengthens the arena of debate with new knowledge. However, what we want from it is more important than all of this: we want it to be the faithful guardian of a people's hopes, to be the vision of tomorrow, perpetual movement, youth renewed, to be the immortal memory of the values of freedom and social justice, and the heart and tongue of eternal revolution.

8 March 1981

AB

A New Phenomenon Called Child Disappearance

Since relatively recently, not less than a year and not more than two years, I have noticed that the press has been publishing the same news item so often that it has attracted attention and deserves a little consideration. It seemed to be a regular news item about the disappearance of an infant or a child, and sometimes a boy or girl teenager, accompanied by a photograph, with the request for anyone who might have seen the missing child to contact his or her family. As I have stated, it is a regular news item which can appear at any time or any place. After a few days a new piece appears about another disappearance and the reader may recall having read something similar previously and skip over it because such items appear so often. It appears a third, a fourth and a fifth time, and then becomes something that almost takes on a weekly rhythm, like a regular advertisement. It catches your attention and sets you thinking now that it has become a social phenomenon that covers up some sort of mirage which needs to be looked into. It goes without saying that every incident of a missing child has been brought to the attention of the authorities who are looking into the matter. However, we demand that these disappearances should be looked at from a different point of view, that they are not separate instances but part of a worrying and highly puzzling phenomenon to which we should accord due concern for reasons of public security and in order to reassure the public.

12 March 1981

RH

When Will the Eradication of Illiteracy Be Completed?

An important conversation has been taking place recently about the eradication of illiteracy and about what has been spent on this important aspect of our lives in terms of effort, organisation and funds. The programme to eradicate illiteracy is very old; we thought about it and legislated for it in the period preceding the Revolution.[1] Not only have we not managed to realise it, but I read now and then that the illiteracy ratio is rising year on year.

After the education reforms, an illiterate person is at an even greater disadvantage and feels even more alienated from the desired society of tomorrow. Although I do recognise the great effort made on trying to eradicate illiteracy, I am well aware that this effort will not achieve its aims as long as general education does not take in every last child in both the rural and urban areas. Had we drafted a robust and all-inclusive education policy years ago, illiteracy would have been wiped out within two generations at the most, without even the need for any special programme to deal with adult illiteracy. When it comes to the continuing attention paid to eradicating illiteracy with its complacency about taking in every child, the results, despite all the effort and the funding, will show no more than a small decrease in the illiteracy ratio. Let us concentrate, above all, on increasing the number of schools for general education so that they take in every child. That is how we will assure the eradication of illiteracy and the provision to every Egyptian

1 The July Revolution in 1952.

of one of his most important human rights which is a right that society will benefit from even more than the individual.

19 March 1981
RH

The University and Intellectual Leadership

Studying at university is essentially specialist studying. Thus, a university provides the student with complete preparation for practising a specific branch of human knowledge. A student is supposed to be accepted at university after completing some general studies. At high school, a student should be directed towards general culture, with the authority of the teacher being able to give him an all-round education. The student should develop his or her general-studies knowledge during his or her free time, and particularly during the summer holidays. This does not stop the university from having a role in general culture and working in close cooperation with cultural institutions in the provinces. The university should provide general lectures, teach students how to participate in debates, and offer students the opportunity to go on trips, hold discussions and organise meetings with leading intellectual figures in the various branches of knowledge.

The phenomenon of intellectual leaders who graduated in the thirties and forties is a perceptible historical phenomenon. By way of example, the university teaching endeavours of Taha Hussein were just part and parcel of his regular activities, and the same goes for Mustafa 'Abd al-Raziq[1] and Mansur Fahmy.[2] This phenomenon moreover is exemplified by teachers of pure science such as Dr Ali Musharafa[3] who

1 Mustafa 'Abd al-Raziq (1885–1947), Islamic philosopher.

2 Mansur Fahmy (1886–1959), Egyptian sociologist and intellectual reformer.

3 Dr Ali Moustafa Mosharafa Pasha (1898–1950), Egyptian theoretical physicist.

worked to educate the new generation and who, at the same time, brought about a general revolution in intellectual life.

Regrettably, this type of activity has diminished markedly in recent years and there is no way we can avoid noticing this. The retreat of the universities and their estrangement from the intellectual field is not due, in my opinion, to the consciences of those with talent but to the general climate.

The thirties were a period when world culture flourished and started to become globalised. Those years witnessed an emphasis on the teaching of foreign languages, the opening of a large number of general bookshops, in addition to a decrease in the price of books, and the increasing interest of leading Egyptian intellectuals in introducing their students to world thought.

We cannot throw the whole burden onto the universities or carry all the responsibility ourselves, for the responsibility of producing intellectual leaders and opinion makers in this country is a task that should begin during the first stages of education. Even if the students or university teachers do not thereafter take up a specialisation, they will still have gleaned enough information and vision to enable them to have an active view on everything that takes place around them.

I believe that there are enough budding young people who have appeared in the intellectual field over the last few years for us to hope that we will be able to get the universities back to offering their students an intellectual adventure as they did in the thirties.

19 March 1981

RH

Freedom of Thought

Freedom is a lofty hope which man does not tire of striving toward, to the extent that civilisation appears sometimes as though it is a struggle between necessity and man's desire for freedom at all its levels: at that of the individual, the collective, and the spiritual. However, each type of freedom has its conditions and disciplines so as to be good for man and pure. Freedom of belief is conditional upon non-hostility towards the beliefs of others, freedom of conduct is conditioned by morals and values, and economic freedom is restricted – or should be – by non-exploitation, and so on, with the exception of freedom of thought. I have not been convinced that this should be impeded by restrictions or bound by conditions. That is to say, its first and last goal is truth – a truth which is indivisible, one part of which will not dispense with the other, and which man cannot possibly overlook, for it is the basis of his life, his survival, and his wealth.

Of course, this does not mean that free thought never errs, but there is no means of correcting thought other than by thought itself, and there is no role here for any external force. Thinking is an arduous task and a serious charge; it demands patience, exertion, and ingenuity. Therefore, why do we further burden it so with artificial restrictions and arbitrary conditions? We continue to import knowledge, its theories and applications, we gasp at its discoveries, but we have contributed hardly anything worth mentioning to world thought. It is incumbent upon us to believe in freedom of thought, to support it, and to free it from limitations and conditions.

26 March 1981

AB

National University

On 30 March 1981 I read for the first time about the new National University, with teaching expected to start at the beginning of the next academic year. I also read that its teaching materials will be directly related to our development programmes, such as the provision of data relating to the improvement of agricultural land, farming, fish farming, poultry and cattle husbandry, the manufacture of agricultural products, meat production and new technologies in the manufacture of ready-made clothing – all of this costs money, of course. I thought that these subjects were actually subjects for agricultural colleges and other teaching institutions. If they are not being taught there, then they could be gradually introduced to the extent possible, meaning that they would be studied in as wide an area as possible and across the governorates. That would be better than establishing a new university whose benefits are restricted to students from one place, i.e., where it is going to be built, and to a group of citizens to the exclusion of others, i.e., those without the means to pay for their education. Development is a duty that goes to building up social solidarity and should not, in the slightest way, go against the principles that we are proud of, such as socialism and social harmony, and which we have set up as a firm basis for our political life.

4 April 1981
RH

Our Language in the Media

From time to time the problem of Arabic on television flares up with comments about how it is presented to the public replete with grammatical mistakes and pronunciation errors, how mistakes spread over the widest possible area by dint of the power of television and its hegemony over our emotions and tastes. This has been discussed in the past in the Supreme Council of the Broadcasting Union, and among the things suggested to resolve it is that male and female broadcasters should take a special course in Arabic. That is a solution about which I feel lukewarm – and at that time I sat on that committee – because any results will only be realised over the long term and then perhaps not in the manner we desire, particularly because none of the broadcasters are starting from zero knowledge but have all studied Arabic for no less than twelve years before embarking on their professional life. Bad Arabic started to spread in the aftermath of the Islamic conquests, and it afflicted the pure Arabs themselves after they migrated and started intermixing with the populations of the territories newly conquered for Islam. I would suggest, as a cure for the problem, that the television should appoint an advisor, or advisors, with language expertise, and that a newsreader should read to him or her the material he is about to broadcast in classical Arabic. The advisor should correct him where necessary, and the newsreader's grammar will be fixed in the quickest way possible. Experience has shown me that this is an easier and more feasible way of correcting errors in reading Arabic aloud. The newsreader will then have no objection to having a handy grammar book nearby in order to check any words he or she is unsure about.

Actually this is a seriously important matter, and the role of the state media should be to set an example of good pronunciation and grammatically correct Arabic.

9 April 1981
RH

The Path to a Real Rebirth

Behind every cultural rebirth is a general principle or notion which appeals to hearts and minds and unites everybody, or a majority of people, around one aim. If that does not come about, people become fissiparous and go their own way; self-interest comes to the fore and everyone acts according to his own whims. That does not mean that human activity or ambition comes to a standstill, but that people restrict themselves to their own personal achievements and the general social spirit becomes diluted. Neither of these can bring about a general and unified cultural rebirth, encourage people to set a supra-personal aim, or buy in to the notion of cultural rebirth. Opinions may vary as to the nature and degree of high mindedness or ethics one should display, but these elements are an unavoidable necessity for uniting people around one aim and for leading them down the long and troublesome road towards cultural rebirth. At one point in time, the cause of Egyptian cultural rebirth was the banner uniting us, and at another point, democracy was our aim, but what is the aim around which we can gather today? Should it be our current war against underdevelopment and our participation in academic and cultural creativity and inventiveness? Should it be the endeavour to bring about a more comprehensive nationalism which can create a more secure and stable country for us? But why should we grope our way forward by intuition and guesswork? Why don't we let people carry out their own research and choose their own means of expression freely? This would then naturally allow the general principles of research to develop in a natural manner as well as through good planning. This would help us to achieve the sort of existence which our society needs and would channel our human motivation towards a true cultural rebirth, one which is truly worthy of the name itself.

23 April 1981
RH

Art, Politics and Internationalism

The question keeps being asked as to whether art in our country has reached the point where it is ready to be seen on the world stage. If not, why not? When and how will it reach this point? It is as if we have solved all our local, cultural problems, as if there is nothing left to think about or discuss, and as if all we now have to worry about is internationalism and posterity. Previously we had an analogous situation with regard to politics, and we threw ourselves onto the worldwide stage in the period of Muhammad Ali,[1] at a time when we could just about be considered a nation-in-the-making, but we took a step backwards for every forward step we made. That experience was repeated after the July Revolution when we aspired to world leadership but paid no heed to how we might fight poverty, ignorance and disease, and the painful consequences cannot be forgotten.[2] Have we been afflicted with a special Egyptian illness called a desire to be a world power? Our unique position between three continents is what drives us to this way of thinking and has made us attempt to up our profile precipitously. Perhaps our driving ambition to be on top is worthy of some sympathy, but we need to remember that a sound structure always stands on a solid and sound base, and that we should start ameliorating conditions at home before moving on to our dreams of the world at large. Before we train for the world boxing championship, for example, we should

1 Muhammad Ali, ruled Egypt 1805–1848.

2 Mahfouz says 'world leadership', but it was actually leadership of the non-aligned and pan-Arab movement that Egypt strived to achieve.

save the millions from bilharzia and various parasitic infections; before we attempt to play a leading role in the world, we should eradicate poverty, ignorance, tyranny, and corruption at home; before we are nominated for a Nobel Prize, we should eradicate the illiteracy which affects 80 percent of the population, excepting of course the educated class, and we should learn how to read, see and hear. We should equip ourselves for a normal and dignified life in its most basic form so that we may then have ambitions to participate in world championships. We should cut our coat according to our cloth.

30 April 1981

RH

Our Role in Constructing Civilisation

Ever since we have taken up the wish for our own cultural rebirth, we have been discussing how we can bring this about. One group suggests that we need to return to our origins, another group calls for us to give ourselves over to modernity, and another group calls for a middle way which reconciles eternal values with the appropriate elements of modernity, and the discussion flares up again every few years. The question remains the same, the discussion never changes, and the suggestions are the same old suggestions. The truth of the matter is that it keeps repeating itself; life does not stop and wait for us to reach a final opinion, and any comparison between how Egypt was at the beginning of the nineteenth century and how it is at the end of the twentieth century is convincing proof of that. But why does the discussion repeat itself so often? It does so because the progress of Egypt has been neither easy nor happy, but marred by regular murderous frustrations. It is only natural that, with every setback, people look inside themselves and at the circumstances to try and discover the reasons and the causes. It has become only natural that some people diagnose the illness as treachery at root and that others diagnose it as some form of reticence about coming to terms with the modern age. Then the discussion rages anew just as it did the first time. What I note about the repeated discussion is that it hinges on whether we should be true to our own culture or the demands of modernity, leaving people only the option of some alternative or an accommodation of the two concepts. I note also that the discussion is about a form of cultural rebirth that somehow comes about without any noteworthy human effort, whereas any true rebirth has to stem from people's spiritual, intellectual and organisational contribution. Being true to our own values or coming to terms with modernity or some accommodation of these two concepts are not the benchmarks by which we should choose what to do or what not to do. The only benchmark should be a concept's usefulness in creating a better life, and we can discover this benchmark within ourselves, with our own strengths and free will as we attempt to deal with our reality, day by day and hour by hour. When it comes to our own values or modernity, these are both vital experiences from which we should derive benefit when the need arises and upon which we should be able to draw freely without an implication of submission or defeat.

7 May 1981

RH

A Bright Light on a Dark Night

I have heard that the play *al-Ustadh* by Sa'd al-Din Wahba[1] achieved great popularity as well as artistic success thereby putting an end to the doldrums in which the theatre has long floundered. We had blamed these doldrums on the financial austerity which the serious theatre public had been passing through and which led to people spending their evenings at home in front of the television. This also meant that a great proportion of the younger generations have suffered from poor cultural education. However, the success of *al-Ustadh* shows clearly that the public can still create an artistic success for the theatre, and perhaps even more if they find something to arouse their interest, and stimulate their minds and emotions. Critics and intellectuals should study this play to determine the reasons for its success. Perhaps the stagnation of which we complain is not due to the reasons we imagined, or is not due to those reasons alone, but can be traced to changing tastes and attitudes, and the need for a new voice and a new tone in the theatre.

We are waiting for Sa'd al-Din Wahba's colleagues, as well as those in the younger generation, to benefit from his success and try their luck so that serious theatre can not only regain its rightful place but also bring a sense of balance back to our theatrical lives, whether in popular or serious theatre. Moreover, why should those outstanding playwrights not pander a little to the masses? I do not mean that they should vulgarise their output but they might offer the public the type of

1 Sa'd al-Din Wahba (1925–1997), Egyptian playwright and theatre director.

comedy they love so that they do not see theatre as something stodgy or heavy. That is what Charlie Chaplin did in his last masterpieces, and so did Naguib el-Rihani.[2] In return for these legitimate concessions, we will be able to hear these playwrights' thoughts and visions, and they will be undertaking the commendable work of developing and reviving stage drama. They will finally put an end to this sharp theatrical divide between the serious and the vulgar, or at least narrow the gap. Is this not an ambition worthy of writers who have emerged from the masses and devoted themselves to them?

14 May 1981

RH

2 Naguib el-Rihani (1889–1949), Egyptian actor of both stage and film.

The Trinity of Intellect, Freedom and Conscience

Since time immemorial the system in our country has been founded on a strong central government which leads, rules, legislates, and is active in all spheres of activity, governing a population which responded and obeyed, whose private lives were not their own. The disadvantages of this system became apparent when the masses came to realise that they were not playing a leading role in their own destiny. With the age of democratisation, the Egyptian masses were not backward about coming forward, sometimes rebelling, sometimes rising up in revolt, but never escaping from frustration after frustration as a result of various local and international causes. Even the July Revolution, which came about for the sake of the people, was a curse upon the masses in its early period. The Revolution strengthened the state apparatus to the nth degree and set the people's optimism back to zero. For that reason, important elements for the construction of our character, such as the intellect and general freedom of conscience, disappeared, or almost disappeared, but these are elements which become stronger as the people's sense of positivity grows and which become weaker or moribund when the people are in a state of negativity.

In our general life, the intellect plays a paltry role. It is as if we live through our feelings and emotions and are offended by freedom, so we fight against it. For that reason, we are wary of experimentation and adventures, we condemn new thinking, and shun situations which need us to take decisions, as if they are a burden which has nothing to do with us. Of the general consciousness, nothing remains but a hackneyed and repeated slogan. Every individual is completely taken up in his own private affairs and concerns, and follows his own personal ambitions. Indeed the intellect, freedom and general conscience are elements which are no longer components in our make-up. People interested in rebuilding the ideal Egyptian should think long and hard about that. In providing a diagnosis they should not restrict themselves to education, the media, and culture, for the problem essentially stems from the system of government, from the reciprocal relationship between the state and the people. For the 15th of May to be a real revolution,[1] it must run its revolutionary course with no hesitation or delay.

21 May 1981

RH

1 That is, Sadat's Corrective Revolution.

The Goal, the Action, and the Example

Every era has a general goal that requires an example of action and conduct that it aims toward and fulfils. It is not enough to invoke this example of action by means of a good word and rational instruction; rather, it must be embodied in a guiding example and be repeated among the leaders of society, then – and only then – will the good word be enacted and the instruction have its impact. The example will come to be commonly adopted among the people and its fruits will be reaped whether it takes a long time or a short one. For example, in the early period of Islam, jihad was the goal in order to spread the message. The required action was courage and sacrifice. The example appeared in the prophet and his companions, and the success appeared as a miracle. We find another example in the 1919 Revolution when Egypt was determined to gain its independence. The struggle arose between a small, defenceless nation and the greatest empire known to history, so resorting to force on the part of Egypt was out of the question. Therefore, the action required was sacrifice, and this was embodied in the leader of the Revolution, the venerable gentleman who said, 'Let the armed force do to us what it will'.[1] He was exiled, the people were moved by the example, and his revolution erupted.

We will encounter this strong correlation between goal, action, and example in every era of construction throughout history, beginning

1 Mahfouz does not provide a reference for the quote, or even quotation marks, for that matter. However, given the context here, it seems quite clear that he is citing Saad Zaghloul (1859–1927), the Egyptian revolutionary and statesman.

from the era of the construction of the pyramids to that of the Second World War. Perhaps it is good that we ask ourselves about the goal of this period of our life. I do not think that there is a difference in that it is the construction of our burdened nation in all its dimensions. There is no difference regarding what this requires in terms of knowledge, action, solidarity, and veracity. There is also no difference regarding the kind of example that should be embodied by the leaders in their various positions. In this way, the good word will become its meaning and its effect, the people will respond to the call, and the miracle will be realised again.

28 May 1981

AB

A Voice That Should Be Heard

In the national councils they are attempting to construct an inclusive image for the future, based on reality, expertise, and science. They study and think about all the relevant fields, from agriculture, manufacturing, and teaching to culture and services. Then they issue recommendations which are sent on to the higher authorities to be implemented. Of all this, the people know almost nothing. From time to time, some decision is published with no further comment or discussion. Furthermore, there is a question which has been occupying me and many other people: Why are these studies and recommendations not publicised as widely as possible among intellectuals and the youth along with a call for a debate on the matter in the press and the other forms of media? These studies represent a serious step in subjecting the nation's problems to solutions which have been suggested. Publicising them would be a good opportunity for national education and the spiritual cohesion of the youth and their hopes for the future, as well as a strong motive for criticism and intellectual inclusion, in which people of various opinions and of all ages could eagerly take part. This would bring about a general and intellectual discussion, which is something we should really strive for, and which would earn popular support from those parties whose interests coincide with our hopes for the future.

4 June 1981

RH

Towards a Free Society

If you want to discover your attitude towards freedom then do not search for it in the extent of your love for it; no one loves it like the despot loves it – he who indulges his love of it to the point of excluding others from it. Instead, look for it in how you deal with your adversary, or contrary views and beliefs. Do you fight them with impartiality and objectivity? Do you prepare the means for their defence and attack as you would for your own? Do you consider truth to be the goal, not triumph or conceit? That which holds true for the individual holds true for the society. Thus, the free society deserves that its House of Representatives mirrors its reality with its various currents, each according to its strength – no more and no less. It is that in which no opinion is stifled or suppressed, whose laws have respect for its creative and innovative powers and, in a word, it is a society that is sound in its senses, mind, and spirit, which works in solidarity and beneath the banner of freedom to strengthen its positive aspects and overcome its negative ones. With its vision it looks toward a future of development and growth – not an end to it. It avoids violent shocks through its wisdom, its good conduct, and its devotion to eternal values. Since the May 15 revolution we have realised achievements in the sphere of democracy that no one will deny; however, it is to our benefit that we re-examine ourselves from time to time, critique ourselves, aspire to perfection, and narrow the gap between what is and what should be.

11 June 1981

AB

Treasure Waiting to Be Discovered

Serious work that is the fruit of scientific endeavour and authentic expertise, carried out in august silence, this is what the Egyptian Association for Culture has been carrying out, year after year. It has been spreading its message in publications in an attempt to deal with the problems of the present day. Were it not for three books which the learned Dr Kamel Mansur gave to me as an example of the sort of studies the Association commissions, I would not have been able to examine the creative effort of these important studies. By way of example, the most important subjects are, in short, the future of agriculture and nutrition in Egypt, technology, disease and cures, various opinions on the topic of family planning, the culture of Egypt between yesterday and tomorrow, along with other deeply significant topics which are too numerous to list here.

It is no surprise that these topics are the subject of discussion among the intelligentsia, but their follow-up, study and the presentation of their results should be subject to the widest dissemination among the people and the various media so that they can reach all levels of society. These and similar works, published by the Association year after year, should be part and parcel of the standard reference works used by the committees of the upper and lower houses of parliament, and the National Council. They should be distributed to popular associations in order to raise the level of scientific consciousness and get people thinking in new ways. Newspapers should devote as many column inches to them as they do to sport and the arts. And last but not least, I call upon television to think about broadcasting them and holding debates with the authors combining interest with gravity, thereby providing the audience with a scientific, cultural, national and liberal education in one fell swoop. In truth, Egypt does have treasures but they are still waiting to be discovered.

18 June 1981
RH

Egypt and Japan

There is a fact which deserves thinking about, and which has often been presented as an enigma by intellectuals over recent years, and that is that Egypt started its cultural rebirth some few years before Japan. So how has Japan reached its outstanding level of development and how have we been subject to this tangible delay? On the one hand, we must discard any reasons associated with racism, and on the other hand it cannot be denied that we have also contributed to the development of civilisation. It is my belief that this painful truth of our underdevelopment can be explained by two causes. Firstly, our cultural rebirth did not provide the popular leadership with the material and spiritual support it needed in order to become a government which could inspire national cohesion, solidarity or a sense of devotion from the masses. It could not provide an enlightened response to any national or liberal demands, and we need no more proof of that than the fact that 80 percent of the population, to this day, are still mired in illiteracy. Secondly, our geographic location between three continents has made us the target of powers striving to control the world.

Due to the lack of inspired government, our cultural rebirth has not gone smoothly, in contrast to Japan, and due to our geographic position various states frustrated the ambitions of Muhammad Ali, just as they frustrated the ambitions of Ismail,[1] and of Gamal Abdel Nasser. We should attempt to draw some benefit from studies of the near and

1 Ismail Pasha (1830–1895), Khedive of Egypt and the Sudan (1863–1879) until he was removed at the behest of the United Kingdom.

distant past and grant our people full custody of their own affairs. We should avoid rising to provocation or challenge and, instead, spend some time in a period of introversion or hibernation, so that we can lick our wounds and open ourselves up to learning, the culture of work, culture itself and values, and never forget that anything devoid of culture is worthless.

25 June 1981
RH

A Secret Trial Is Needed

My address is not directed toward the Muslims and the Copts; their belief in unity is beyond dispute, and their indignation about the reckless events is as one and needs no mention. I am addressing those who are aberrant among the people of El Zawya El Hamra who were blinded by anger or bigotry, or both.[1] I call every individual among them to a secret, personal trial whose scene is his self, and whose witnesses are his heart and his conscience. Let him put his own self on trial, by himself. Was that which issued from him the best that it could have been? Was it the best and most effective remedy? Did its effects arrive as he would have liked and desired? And when he finishes bringing himself to account, I propose to him that he considers – just considers – that he has an obligation to defend his adversary, so that he enter into this with sincerity, for the sake of the experiment. Will he find something in his defence? Is it possible he will even find in his position some truth? And can he even find some excuse for his anger? I demand this of you because I believe that bigotry is an aberrant mental state that has no relation to religion, even if a breathing space for it exists in religion, as we find in sports, or politics, and other such things. It is a pathological state and, like other sicknesses, it requires a doctor, but the person who is ill must fight against the illness. Undertake this secret, mental trial so that you might attain remorse, for the entirety

1 Here Mahfouz is commenting upon the sectarian violence that erupted between Muslims and Christian Copts in the El Zawya El Hamra neighbourhood of Cairo in June 1981.

of dreaded punishments will not be a substitute for remorse – eternal, holy, patriotic remorse.

13 July 1981
AB

The Meaning of Civilisation

How can we judge various civilisations or compare them? Perhaps we can find the rational answer to that by looking at spiritual and material achievements – at what was found to be useful at one time and then disappeared, at what has remained unchanged across the vicissitudes of time, and at what has been imported into other cultures and has developed and continued in a new form. That is the way civilisations arise over the course of history and what has made them give rise to admiration, wonder and criticism. It is perhaps the material aspect which has aroused special interest, not because of the material objects themselves but because of their weighty influence on the one hand, and the speed of their ramifications on the other hand as a result of people's willingness to interact and derive benefit from material objects, even though the material output of civilisations has not caused the same astonishment, esteem, and unlimited admiration that modern industry and technology have awakened.

I believe that there is another aspect in comparative cultures which is represented in ordinary individuals in a society and which is particular to them; it is to be found within the people in whom a civilisation is embodied in all its good and bad aspects, and they are the truest witnesses to it. They are witnesses to that aspect of a civilisation in the way they conceive of existence, life, and other people. They are witnesses to it in terms of their physical, intellectual, and psychological health, witnesses to what makes their hearts pulse with happiness or sadness, in their creative and moral energies, and, last but not least, in terms of their selflessness, sense of respect and their social relations with other people no matter whether they differ in terms of colour, language, or belief, or in all of these. This judgment of mine should elicit no surprise, as civilisation has come into existence for the sake of human beings and not vice versa.

16 July 1981

RH

We Are Born Egyptian

We are born Egyptian. This attribute cleaves to our souls and bodies the moment we exit the womb and our bodies touch the ground. But it goes back further than this; it goes back to the loins of our fathers and forefathers, and, hence, we are born Egyptian. As we go through life we grow and acquire new attributes, some of which we agree with and some we do not. We acquire these through nurture, education, socialisation, culture or self-interest, and though our schools of thought or belief, our tastes and ways of seeing, are many, we remain Egyptian. We may disagree with each other so much that a brother disowns his brother, friends may argue with each other, a neighbour may enter into a dispute with his neighbour, we may all disagree over what is realistic or not, what we should do today or tomorrow, over a disease and its treatment, or over phrases and meanings, but we all remain Egyptian. We might take extreme positions on a subject, or resort to hyperbole and become overexcited, we might sink into bad ways of behaviour, but, despite all that, we all remain Egyptian. It is not simply an adjective, but in truth it is a life, a shelter and a sanctuary, a beginning and an end. It is the ship which carries us all through good and bad times. We have the right to differ with each other; this is only natural and a sign of freedom and freethinking. It is our right to argue and to be competitive, and every group has the right to realise its own way of seeing things, but it is also our right and our duty to remember where we come from, to remember the principle that we should remember the ship, and anything that neither scuttles the ship nor stops it from sailing ever on should be permitted.

23 July 1981
RH

Creative Intelligence

Humans have many forms of activity which are worthy of esteem and admiration, but it is our creative energy which is more exciting and wonderful than any of our other capabilities. Man is an innovative creature in the fields of science and art and has innate values which have enabled him to create civilisations and to be inspired with hope, despite humanity having lived through various dark periods in our development. This fact should not be absent for a moment from the minds of those state officials in charge of our new educational rebirth. They speak at great length about making good use of the labour force, about its distribution and equipping it for the five-year development plan, and the needs of society and the environment.

That is a very prudent and successful vision, but it must pivot on an important focal point which is that of intelligence. And how do we nurture the intelligence to be free and independent, to think and innovate, and not just to follow old ways of thinking? How do we nurture human intelligence to face the world with confidence, to realise its capacities and move forward without being hampered by underdevelopment or overcome by obtuseness, to give as much as it takes, to guide as it has been guided and to provide judgment as well as to pass on wisdom? A nation prospers to the extent that it creates, and creativity is more important than ease, comfort or raw materials. Creativity is a magical state, and when it is allowed to breathe it broadcasts its voice indifferent to the suffocating atmosphere around it and laws which attempt to fetter it.

30 July 1981

RH

Thought between the Predecessor and the Successor

People ask a lot about what has happened to thought. Why are there no longer outstanding intellectuals such as el-Akkad, Taha Hussein, and Ali Abdel Raziq,[1] not to mention a plethora of others?

The truth is that we have not been afflicted by barrenness in human productivity and that among us there are many people whose high level of scientific knowledge has surpassed that of their predecessors and who have achieved more, or gone beyond the thinking capacity of their forefathers. So, where are the flights of thought in philosophy, society and culture? The issue is that these early thinkers lived in a climate which sanctified freedom and who were proud to work away night and day. Even those who saw political freedom as something for which the country was not ready were at the forefront of those calling for freedom of expression in the fields of culture and civilisation. The most that would happen to an intellectual if he overstepped the boundary in the opinion of society was that he would face the judiciary, who were, for their part, leading elements in admiring the truths brought about by intellectual activity. Contemporary intellectuals, however, are now living in a different climate – one which places the system above freedom, one which calls for a monolithic society, restricts free thinking and cannot tolerate dissidents. People now have to work within that framework and keep their ideas to themselves as well as finding

1 Ali Abdel Raziq (1888–1966), Islamic scholar, religious judge and government minister.

that more and more of their time is taken up dealing with the necessities of daily life – something caused by rampant inflation.

Today we hope that everything will change following the Corrective Revolution of 15 May, with the fate of culture and thought now lying in the hands of the intellectuals themselves.

6 August 1981

RH

Peace between Action and Thought

One of the principles upon which our social system is founded is that of peace between the classes, in the sense that it caused solidarity between the classes to take the place of the struggle that other systems believe in. Success beneath the shelter of this principle depends upon every citizen's devotion to it and the endeavour to achieve it through honesty and trust – otherwise it will revert to being a slogan without meaning and a mask behind which hide exploitation, greed, and opportunism.

At any rate, we can aspire to social peace within the sphere of work, but as for the world of thought, it has a particular nature that is not compatible with peace; rather, perhaps peace in the world of thought means only languor and lethargy, then death. This is because thought is only active, enthusiastic, and inventive through struggle, discord, and provocation.

Throughout history, our greatest intellectual achievements have only ever come about through intellectual battles raging within religion, philosophy, and literature. Denying access to some of the elements of thought, and depriving them of breath and expression, cleared the field of the ingredients of stimulation and provocation, and left legitimate elements of thought alone in the arena, jumping and roaming aimlessly. Their passion cooled, their determination waned, and their spirit became extinguished. In other words, whoever denies access to a portion of thought denies access to thought in its entirety.

13 August 1981

AB

To You, the Real Accused

Much accusation has been levelled against the state television service over its responsibility for firing many of its newsreaders and for not presenting serious culture. This calls us to wonder about the stance which we should take regarding recent innovations in the field of culture. Should we demand an end to innovation in case it undermines our previous achievements? In the normal course of events we cannot hold back the tide. We do not have the power to make human imagination stop creating, nor to tie civilisation or culture down to some stake beyond which it should not go. People must innovate and the new must be allowed to flourish. We must come to terms with the new in order to make it serve our interests and those of humanity.

The truth is that the state television service is not responsible for firing those newsreaders. The responsibility falls upon us, for we have not equipped our children with sufficient cultural resilience to enable them to appreciate the television without it having a damaging effect on reading and serious culture. We are the ones who have not provided our children with the necessary education, and we are the ones who have deprived our children of the free and healthy climate needed for thought and artistic endeavour to flourish. Hence, when television came along it found our children ready victims, optimally predisposed to be totally overwhelmed by an addiction to television's entertainment programmes rather than any serious cultural programming. That is the problem in a nutshell. It is inherent in us, not in the television. We must carry out our duty to ourselves and our children, and we must prepare them to face life appropriately. That is how the television will become a beacon for culture, with light entertainment just a supplement to our spiritual lives. That is how we can avoid suffering the loss of the loftier values we so treasure.

20 August 1981
RH

The Golden Age of the Magazine

It appears that it will be a long time before we can find the cure for our cultural stagnation. Opinion is united on books being the first point of reference for serious culture, just as opinion is united on the point that the crisis can be resolved by the Book Authority, its branches, cultural centres and other institutions providing low-cost books to readers, or through cheap popular editions or some other means. However, as I have said, it appears that it will be a long time before we can pass legislation to put this into action, and as the matter will probably take such a long time, I would suggest that we give special serious attention to magazines. A serious cultural magazine can take the place of a book, even if only to a certain degree, by making it a conduit for disseminating what is happening in the world around us in terms of new trends in scientific thought, philosophy, literature and the arts. Magazines can do the job of many serious books and be sold at a price which is not a burden to the overwhelming majority of people who seek to improve themselves. This is not demanding the impossible of us. We just have to revitalise existing magazines, or start up a new quality magazine devoted to general culture and appearing in weekly instalments. In this regard, we might also care to remember that our generation received its cultural education from weekly and monthly magazines. There were not many books around at that time but there was a plethora of serious magazines in whose pages heated intellectual battles raged, artistic and cultural trends clashed, and which overflowed with information about our ancient culture and offered us contemporary thought from the world outside. These magazines were our gateway to maturity, our guidebooks to the world of thought, literature and art. As long as the book-publishing industry remains in a parlous state, and for all that we might talk and get nothing done, why should we not revive the 'magazine experience' and that golden age which provided immeasurable benefits at a cost of peanuts?

27 August 1981

RH

Sedition and Corruption

The newspapers have announced that the president will make an important statement concerning the sectarian sedition the day after tomorrow – Saturday – and that he is determined to tackle it at its roots, just as he is determined to eradicate corruption and cleanse the country of its woes. We await this with hearts full of hope, convinced that the president has examined the apparent and the underlying causes of the sedition, and that he will deal with each cause accordingly in pursuit of a national and humanitarian goal about which there is no dispute: that each citizen enjoys safety and security, peace and love, and that each performs his duties and exercises his rights in an atmosphere of absolute equality worthy of Egypt and its glorious history and ancient pedigree. Perhaps corruption was not linked to sedition by coincidence, for they are twins. Corruption is nothing more than the dissolution of principles, a flight from faith in belonging, and the surrender to lust, selfishness, and opportunism. Thus, it will hatch any evil, degrade any value, and exploit any human being; it is not free from any negative behaviour, be it the death of a citizen in a hospital, a violation of traffic laws, or an act of hostility against a church or a mosque.

The truth is that we are waiting with hearts full of hope, and we are eager for that which will bring us complete unity and true earnestness. Moreover, we are eager for everything that will enable us to tackle the era with its complex problems and its difficult requirements. Let us entrust reconciliation to the president and stand prepared to respond and participate.

3 September 1981

AB

Unity between Preparation and Construction

We are certain now that the resolutions made on the matter of sectarian sedition have confronted, with a genuine resolve, its direct causes and its complications, just as they have provided a good environment for the restoration of equilibrium to those filled with agitation and mistrust. However, they have not spoken the final word regarding the situation. Perhaps they are only the preparation that precedes construction, or the prelude that leads to the goal. The construction and the goal are none other than the establishment of the lofty edifice of a healthy society whose fabric will be composed of exalted humanitarian values, which peace and justice will govern, which faith in human rights and science will underpin, and which the spirit of citizenship and love will lead in the journey of progress. This brings us back to the issue of re-examining the construction of the Egyptian character; the role of the Ministry of Education in arranging true religious education and sound patriotic education; the role of the media – the press, radio, and television – in establishing these principles and spreading them through their engaging means, through interviews, reports, and drama; and the role of the state which holds the scales of justice and equality, and which, ultimately, sets the example for people to follow. I very much wanted my discourse to include the resolutions on corruption in order to complete the siege of the malady and facilitate its elimination. I await these with the impatience of a citizen who always yearns for a better tomorrow.

10 September 1981

AB

Towards the Paradise of National Unity

We must make a distinction between sectarianism and sectarian sedition. Sedition is a recent phenomenon of aberrant, sectarian feeling manifested in an abominable, tangible form. As for sectarianism, it is the tyranny of a particular grouping against the general, national sense of belonging. Sectarianism stems from various causes and is united by common characteristics, such as intolerance, injustice, ignorance, and selfishness. Were it not for sectarianism, sedition would not have flared up, even if the direct causes were plentiful, whereas, it is in relation to sectarianism that sedition flares up for the most baseless reasons or for no reason at all.

We hope that the Committee for National Unity investigates the real causes, for there can be no effective treatment without an accurate diagnosis. If only it would employ those means which are simplest and offer the best guarantee, that is, going back to the people themselves, even if by using public questionnaires in field research, along with listening to the opinion makers in the two camps. We are not starting from scratch; we have a long and full history of solidarity, unity, and patriotism, which will make the detection of unforeseen symptoms of disease easy. It will not be time wasted; it will be expended for national unity, and the effort dedicated to it will not be considered as additional in respect to our general burdens, because corruption only infects unity when it has already infiltrated our political, social, or moral life. Ultimately, the committee's task will inevitably be to reform society and life in Egypt.

17 September 1981

AB

The Work Revolution

The press has brought us up to date regarding the recommendations of the National Democratic Party committees – comprehensive recommendations which take into account domestic and foreign policy, and all aspects of development and cultural activities in their material and spiritual forms. The party conference considered these party platforms to be instituted by the government which will be held to account for how it carries them out at the next conference. Furthermore, we read the resolutions regarding party discipline and they were also significant in terms of their seriousness and legitimate ambition. We do not want for thinking or good intentions, and through these resolutions and recommendations we have learnt the path and method we have to follow and what our aims are. We also learnt the bases for realising these aims in the broadest possible ways. Nor do we lack the necessary funds to bring these about, nor the local expertise or the foreign aid, as confirmed by the spokesman on economic affairs. Thus, all we have to do is continue carrying them out, redoubling our efforts and putting as much faith into action as was put into those words. We no longer have the slightest excuse for indecision, sloth, putting things off or ignoring them. We will not be accused of trying to reach for the stars if we demand things to be completed, if we head towards success or pin our hopes on a brighter future. We have striking examples of what we have managed to achieve in the party, such as peace, the reopening of the Suez Canal, and development at a popular level. Through productive, serious and continuous work we shall reaffirm national unity, democracy and social justice, for this is the work of a revolution.

5 October 1981

RH

Eras and Leaders

When we consider this topic, we see a wondrous parallel between conditions in the various historical eras and the essential attributes used to describe the leader controlling that era's destiny, unless the effort of that leader was destined to bring about significant achievements which had an effect on the country's destiny. That becomes clear when we examine the July Revolution over its three periods. During the first period, the country was the prey of colonialism, feudalism and foreign control of the economy. The country needed an unstoppable and relentless will to continue the angry and resolute struggle in order to break free from the shackles of useless traditions, to reform society on new foundations which would give it some equilibrium, justice, and dignity, and to cleave a path through the desert to a new life. It was in Gamal Abdel Nasser that Egypt found the leader it desired. He made great achievements by which he liberated the country from political and economic imperialism and feudal injustice and steered it along the path of social rebirth and energised the nationalism which still pulsates in us today.

In the second period the country was wracked by of a series of bitter defeats. Economic strangulation had led the country to an impasse and brought it to the edge of despair. The country needed a Sufi heart brimming with faith and a vivid imagination which could turn the impossible into the possible. This period found its man in the form of Anwar Sadat, who brought Egypt out from the terror of night into the safety of daylight, from authoritarian rule to bureaucratic rule, from the bitterness of defeat to the pride of victory, from a state of war to a state of peace, and from economic strangulation to the liberalisation of the economy and inward investment. With these achievements, among others, he reinvigorated the youth of the country, breathed new life into its spirit and set it on the path to modernity and affluence.

In the third period the country was backsliding into apathy, sloth and indifference. As a result, there was a dire need for a heart which beats with justice, uprightness, trust and good governance, and a need for a sincere and robust decisiveness capable of action, of inculcating trust among the people, of inspiring them to work, and of bringing back a general sense of order. In other words, there was a dire need for a comprehensive, ethical revolution to inspire new hope. Evidence shows that the nation found its saviour in the person of the new president, as attested by his history, his work and his success in the October War, and by the words he spoke in his first speech in which he gave an overview of his general vision and called upon the nation to work hard and to be disciplined, enthusiastically advocating equality, justice and integrity, making no distinction between rich and poor, between near and far, and rejecting flattery, hypocrisy, idle chatter, treachery, ignorance and indolence. As a result of this speech, the people accepted him wholeheartedly, their hopes were reawakened, and all wished him success in his endeavour. In fact, it is the ethical revolution that we have long been waiting for.

12 October 1981

RH

The Meaning of Stability

If security breaks down for one reason or another, the first and most urgent duty of the state is to use everything at its disposal – weapons, legislation, and surveillance – to put an end to the disturbances, so that the foundations of safety and security are guaranteed. However, this does not signify stability in its profound sense – it is a victory in a battle, not the winning of a war. We must then investigate the hidden causes that induce unrest and aberration. We will find that these causes are what prevent society from becoming a civilised society worthy of the human being. Among these is that which is related to values, and devotion to them in word and deed; that which paves the way for science, work, and a future opened up for our young people; that which will realise justice among the people equally and without discrimination; that which will guarantee man his rights of freedom and dignity; and among them is the creation of a good environment for ideas and objective discussion to come together. In other words, stability is nothing more than what we refer to today as rational development, democracy, regulation, and the decisive assault on corruption and degeneration. The burden of duty requires that the state, the political parties, the media, and every citizen capable of thinking or acting, cooperate in shouldering it. It is not a battle; rather, it is a trajectory whose path has been impeded by the greed of a group of people and the corruption of others. We must propel it with truthfulness and sincerity so that its progress proceeds and its goals are achieved.

29 October 1981

AB

Young People and the Message of Religion

Recently, Al-Azhar called for there to be a dialogue with young people in order to inform them about the true character of their religion. Put simply and clearly, this means that the religious education in schools did not convey its desired message and that there needs to be a review of its decisions and approach. With regard to the task of Al-Azhar, I hope that we bear in mind that religion has two aspects: the theoretical, which comprises the principles, the methods, and the vision; and the practical, which pertains to conduct that the believer must abide by. He must traverse its path in life so that he will attain perfection in his relationship with his being and in his relationship with his community, as he deals with his worldly existence and prepares himself for his hereafter. Of course, the expected outcome is both knowledge and action, that is to say, that the young person knows his religion and that he progresses, with faithfulness and devotion, along the path of practicing and applying it, and that he finds therein the answer to all of the questions that could conceivably be stirred up within his soul, just as he finds the solutions to the hard or difficult problems that may confront him.

Therefore, the preacher must be thoroughly familiar with the mentality of young people, the contemporary currents that surround them, the difficulties and obstacles that threaten their security and their future, the social contradictions that rend them, economic concerns, and sexual and class crises. The preacher must be aware of all of this and, thereby, gain the trust and confidence of young people. There is nothing wrong in him having recourse to the questionnaires of the information bureaus in his work. He should distribute thousands of them so that a register of the young people's concerns and true thoughts will be available to him, then he will know where to begin, what to concentrate on, and what to elaborate on and reiterate. Sirs, we desire you to have an honest, successful dialogue that will please God and his messenger. Indeed, we hope that you broaden the sphere of guidance to include the old – not just the young people. In my opinion they are more in need of your guidance than the young.

5 November 1981

AB

The Only Remedy for Aberration Is Civilisation

We believe that the emergence of aberrant religious groups is fundamentally due to a misunderstanding of religion, according to which society appears as an infidel that deserves to be shunned and punished. This is why the call has arisen for correct religious education as a decisive remedy for the misunderstanding concerning religion and the emergence of aberrant religious groups. But will correct religious education erase the contradiction between religion and society? Will the youngster who receives a correct Islamic education not find a contradiction between the teaching that is instilled in him and that which goes on in his family, his street, his political and economic system, and the various ills which his society suffers from? I believe that this youth will perceive this contradiction and be torn apart by the confusion between what he has learned and the convictions, social relations, and conventions in accordance with which the order of life proceeds. The expected logical outcome is that he will either look down on religion, viewing it as so many fine words that are impracticable in terms of application, or else he will cling to religion and indict society. In the course of his transition he will need wisdom and good spiritual counsel. However, there will always be a group around that will call for extremism or respond with fiery emotions, for it will persist in its attitude until society atones anew and embraces violence and crime. So, in truth, what is the decisive remedy for this situation? In my view, this will only be attained through the purification of society, its alteration, the eradication of its ugly aspect, by pushing it along the path of economic, social and cultural progress, and through respect for human rights, such as justice, freedom, etc. In short, the only remedy for aberration is civilisation. By this the contradiction between correct religious education and society will disappear.

19 November 1981
AB

O God, Protect Our Press for Us![1]

Freedom is not about addressing a new exposition of an opinion, or culture, or a policy, or an institution, only in order to meet it with a ready hostility and a disagreeable, entrenched way of thinking, and so that voices are raised in protest, asking: 'What do you have in mind?', 'What do you mean?', 'What are your hidden intentions?', and 'Does absolute freedom exist?' The proposals rain down with various stipulations, conditions, and consummate skill in conjuring up dangers and concerns until suffocation is firmly seated upon its throne and hearts are set. This is fear of the truth, irritation at the opinion of the other, ossification, inflexibility, fear of change, and the loss of self-confidence. Don't forget that there are lessons for us about this matter in our distant and recent past. Perhaps we would be ten times better off than we are if we were to deal with freedom in a different way than we have.

These thoughts accost me when I think about the eventual outcome concerning the matter of the press after the conclusion of its reform. The press is the eye by which we see, the lung by which we breathe, and the lamp which reveals the truths in the darkness. We desire a discerning eye, a sound lung, and a radiant lamp, so that we have a

---

1 I should note that this piece is not in chronological sequence in the original book, I have repositioned it chronologically here on the assumption that the date given in the original is correct and not a typographical error. See Mahfouz, *Ḥawla l-Dīn wa-l-Dīmūqrāṭīya*, p. 77

rightly-guided life, an unerring journey, and kindliness that is worthy of human beings. O God, protect our press for us!

22 November 1981
AB

Do the Youth Have a Problem?

Let us imagine that a child in our country enjoys parental tenderness at home, good food, and innocent games which stimulate his imagination and creativity, and that he then finds a healthy atmosphere at school and receives good teaching, a rational, religious, nationalist and liberal education, physical exercise and various forms of artistic activity. Let us also imagine that he turns out well and is well equipped for a successful working life in a craft or a profession, and that the future extends in front of him with the promise that his efforts will be crowned with concomitant success and that he will be able to satisfy his essential needs such as marriage, inasmuch as his abilities permit him. Let us also imagine that we change our treatment of him when he reaches adolescence, that we consider him our equal in terms of opinion and discussion, and that we give him his due responsibilities at home and outside it. Let us consider that he will soon learn the elements of leadership, that we will respect his point of view on all political and national matters and that we will allow him the space to express his views and work. Let us imagine thereafter that we have provided him, from our private and public life, with good examples of how to work hard with honour, dignity, and respect for human rights.

If you can imagine that, can you imagine that this child could turn out to be anything other than big-hearted, decent towards other people, and with a sense of pride in his forefathers, his neighbours and his leaders? And can you imagine that if he then falls into bad ways that this must be some form of psychosis for which we would not be able to find a psychiatrist or other type of doctor to cure him?

I would, therefore, say to you that there is no specific problem with our youth. The real problem is the sanctimoniousness of adults who wish to be the movers and shakers of society. The problem is that of the adults and what they create in their society, the good and the bad that they add to it, and the principles they adopt in the way they deal with other people. They are the ones creating the human drama and making it into some sort of epic, black comedy, or bloody tragedy.

May good humble our adults so that our young people can find the right way.

26/11/1981

RH

A Complete Reconsideration

There is no doubt that a new mode of political intercourse is now entering our life, and perhaps it is only natural that we reconsider the basic elements of our society so that harmony can prevail over the opposition and quarrelling between the status quo, on one hand, and this mode, on the other. A critical, constructive reconsideration will aim at correction, modification, and consolidation. It will amount to a careful, new reading of the constitution, the laws, and the institutions, so that the structure is raised up strong and lofty on the foundations of freedom, justice, reason, and faith. It will guarantee us a civilisational launch which will be characterised by persistence, strength, and success. Yet, as soon as the citizen thinks about this he is confronted by the pressing economic and social problems, and worries concerning daily life. He asks himself: Will polarising activity not subject minds and wills to a convulsion if we commence with a complete reconsideration of our affairs? With regard to this I have thought of proposing the following:

Firstly, that, within each ministry, a permanent deputy be assigned to the affairs of the plan whose work will focus upon the implementation of projects and their follow-up, whose full powers are set to work in the event of the government's resignation or when the minister is occupied with the business of committees, the Cabinet, and public administration. The deputy will be answerable for his work to the People's Assembly, for he will submit to it, at the end of session, what has been implemented, what was not implemented, and the reasons for this.

Secondly, that an official people's committee be formed in which all leanings regarding the reconsideration of the prevailing system are represented, with a view to ensuring its strength, progressiveness, and humanitarian values, so that, ultimately, it will propose a comprehensive vision to which everyone will be committed to – a commitment to reverence, loyalty, and implementation.

31 December 1981

AB